Writing for Theatre

Approaches to Writing

Series Editor: Graeme Harper

Published

Craig Batty and Zara Waldeback, *Writing for the Screen*
Amanda Boulter, *Writing Fiction*
Chad Davidson and Greg Fraser, *Writing Poetry*
Jeremy Scott, *Creative Writing and Stylistics*
Kim Wiltshire, *Writing for Theatre*

Forthcoming

Vanessa Harbour, *Writing Young Adult Fiction*

Approaches to Writing
Series Standing Order
ISBN 978-1-4039-9999-3
(*Outside North America Only*)

You can receive future titles in this series as they are published by placing a standing order. Please contact your bookseller or, in the case of difficulty, write to the address below with your name and address, the title of the series and the ISBN quoted above.

Customer Services Department, Macmillan Distribution Ltd,
Houndmills, Basingstoke, Hampshire RG21 6XS, UK

Writing for Theatre

Creative and Critical Approaches

Kim Wiltshire

First published 2016 by
PALGRAVE

Palgrave in the UK is an imprint of Macmillan Publishers Limited,
registered in England, company number 785998, of 4 Crinan Street,
London N1 9XW.

Palgrave Macmillan in the US is a division of St Martin's Press LLC,
175 Fifth Avenue, New York, NY 10010.

Palgrave is a global imprint of the above companies and is represented
throughout the world.

Palgrave® and Macmillan® are registered trademarks in the United States,
the United Kingdom, Europe and other countries.

ISBN 978–1–137–36919–2

This book is printed on paper suitable for recycling and made from fully
managed and sustained forest sources. Logging, pulping and manufacturing
processes are expected to conform to the environmental regulations of the
country of origin.

A catalogue record for this book is available from the British Library.

Library of Congress Cataloging-in-Publication Data
Names: Wiltshire, Kim.
Title: Writing for theatre : creative and critical approaches / Kim Wiltshire.
Description: New York : Palgrave Macmillan, 2016. | Series: Approaches to
    writing | Includes index.
Identifiers: LCCN 2015038906 | ISBN 9781137369192 (paperback)
Subjects: LCSH: Playwriting. | Drama – Technique. | BISAC: LANGUAGE ARTS &
    DISCIPLINES / Composition & Creative Writing. | LITERARY CRITICISM /
    Drama. | PERFORMING ARTS / Theater / Playwriting.
Classification: LCC PN1661 .W55 2016 | DDC 808.2 – dc23
LC record available at http://lccn.loc.gov/2015038906

Printed in China

For the Fabulous Bailey Boys – with love

Contents

Acknowledgements

I would like to thank all the interviewees (all of whom are listed in the Introduction) who agreed to sit down and talk with me, who inspired me with their passion and enthusiasm for theatre and whose participation meant that I could write the book I wanted to write.

Thanks also go to my colleagues at Edge Hill University who supported and advised me from start to finish on this project, and the creative writing students who took time out to read draft sections and tell me if I was going in the right direction for them.

I am also very grateful to Professor Graeme Harper who has been so supportive and encouraging – as well as having many wise and kind words of advice for me when I went off down the wrong path or got myself in a muddle! The team at Palgrave, especially Rachel, have also been fantastic, patient, helpful and reassuring.

Finally, thanks to Craig Bailey for reading, questioning, suggesting and – most importantly – proofing drafts.

Introduction

When I first considered writing a book about writing for theatre, my initial feeling was that, although I write plays, make theatre and teach script writing, I'm not really old enough or experienced enough or famous enough. This is because most books about writing or creating theatre, especially in the UK, are written by the grandees of theatre, usually late on in their careers when they can bestow their hard-won wisdom on us less experienced writers. And there is nothing at all wrong with these books; indeed I very much enjoy reading them (you can find a selection listed in the further reading section at the back of this book). I love finding out what Alan Ayckbourne, David Mamet, Peter Brook and David Edgar, to name but a few, have to say about their experiences of making theatre. Initially, I had no idea what I could possibly add to these wise words from people who were so practised in their craft and had such a wide range of knowledge. So, what changed my mind about writing a book?

Teaching theatre writing to undergraduate students on a creative writing programme.

Many of the new and often young writers I meet in the university seminar room, usually in the first days of their undergraduate creative writing degrees, have very little interest in theatre writing. They want to be novelists or poets or film writers. They think theatre is old fashioned, only to do with pantomime and musicals or Shakespeare and dead, white middle-class male writers. And of course it can be all of those things, but for me it is very much more; it is a passion, a collaborative creative experience and, I believe, the best way to tell a story. This is what I try to get across to these new student writers in the hope that I can help them discover a passion for writing theatre that they never knew they had.

Suzanne Bell, Dramaturg and New Writing Associate at The Royal Exchange, Manchester (don't worry, I am going to explain these terms later), came to talk to some of my first year creative writing students a couple of years ago, and one of the first things she told them was that people who work at making theatre are theatre geeks. They spend their days creating theatre and their evenings watching theatre. They want to know what is going on in the theatre world; they collaborate and enthuse about each other's work. They discuss theatre endlessly, they have their heroes and their villains, and they can probably bore non-theatre makers to distraction with their enthusiasm.

Listening to her talk to these young and emerging writers, I realised she was describing me. I am no grandee of theatre, simply a self-confessed theatre geek who wants to share that passion. And that urge to share is part of what making theatre is all about. Even though I teach script writing, I am still learning as a playwright and always will be – learning is a continuous process for most writers, I would suggest. But for writers new to playwriting I believe that one of the first things you need to acknowledge is that to write well for theatre, you have to become a theatre geek, and reading this book is hopefully your first step on the first rung of the theatre geek ladder.

To learn to be a theatre geek, then, there are a few basics you must accept before even thinking of writing your first line of scripted dialogue.

Firstly, theatre is a collaborative medium. Secondly, a playwright must engage their critical as well as their creative mind. Thirdly, a playwright must understand what theatre is, what it can do as a medium as well as what it can't do. And finally, a playwright must understand how all of this affects the paying audience.

Collaboration

Theatre's very nature is collaborative. As a playwright, the script you are writing should be seen as a plan or a blueprint or an instruction manual for the eventual production that can only come about through collaboration with other artists; a play never lives on the page. During the performance the play will then collaborate with the audience to create a show that will never be exactly the same twice; each night a new piece of art will be created between the cast, technicians and audience. It is a way of working that over time becomes second nature, although at first it can seem quite daunting.

When it came to deciding how I could write this book for those students of creative writing who are new to theatre, the idea struck me that it too should be collaborative. Of course I could simply tell you what I think about creating theatre as a writer, but I wanted to give a more rounded view. I am lucky enough to work with so many great theatre makers who are making new theatre work *now*, so I asked them to share with me their passion for theatre. I interviewed writers, directors and dramaturgs, asking them about their process, their theories and philosophies around creating theatre, their opinions on where theatre currently sits in the cultural landscape, and where it might be heading, as well as their thoughts on the process and craft of playwriting.

Through these interviews I aim to give you, the theatre geek in the making, a sense of what making theatre in these early decades of the twenty-first century is really like, as well as where, in your hands, it could be going.

And there is another reason why I am not simply giving you my opinion on what makes good theatre writing, or giving you a range of exercises to create characters or plots; there are many excellent books out there already that can do this (and again I have listed a few of these at the back). But the majority of these books assume one thing: that the reader already understands or at least has a good grounding in theatre and perhaps is already writing for theatre. But what if you are a totally new writer and you are not quite at that stage? Often these books can seem discouraging, they can create a mystique around the craft and critical theories of creating theatre which can only fully be grasped once the emerging writer is secure in their own desire to write and create theatre.

So, whilst some classic plays and grandees may be referred to by the interviewees here, for the most part I will concentrate on new writing for the simple reason that you, the new playwright, will be entering the world of new writing yourself.[1] Whilst it is important that an emerging playwright has an understanding of theatre history as a basis on which to build, knowing what new theatre is happening, or could be happening, enables you to explore the many possibilities for creating exciting theatre.

This book will therefore discuss both the creative and critical aspects of making theatre, because to understand how to make theatre well, you must engage with it critically, you must analyse craft on both the page and the stage, and you must engage critically with the wider world around you.

Critical engagement

The critical aspects of this book then fall into two areas. The first is an understanding of what has gone before, and this is explored through the chapters on theatre history and innovators. It is important to critically engage with what has gone before in theatre because so much new theatre often has a sense of intertexuality with its past, whether it be through a revival of a type of Greek chorus or through references to specific famous moments in theatre, or even simply building on aspects of story, form or style. The second area is the critical engagement with the world around you, both the theatre world and the wider world, and how this can affect the writer creatively.

---

[1] Although this is often a problematic term in the theatre world, as some interviewees will point out – but in terms of defining 'new writing' for this book I am meaning the phrase literally – writing that is new.

Theatre can often be a very political arena. Of course you may read that and think: How political are most musicals? How political are 1970s farces? How political are most of the plays out there – surely they are good old-fashioned entertainment? I would certainly agree that theatre has to be entertaining; however I would argue that analytical or critical engagement with the wider world around you on a series of levels is, and always has been, crucial for the playwright. Knowing what is happening in the world politically, culturally and creatively allows the playwright to ask bigger questions of the story they choose to tell, bigger questions of their audience, and to explore new ways of using theatre, and even new theatre forms, to do this.

Because theatre is collaborative many of the more theoretical or critical books on theatre are often written not by playwrights at all, but by dramaturgs and directors, the ones who usually work on the creation of the actual production and so perhaps engage more with the various movements and fashions that come and go in theatre. These trends often move in cycles linked to varying political or cultural movements, however I believe that to be a good playwright, a writer must also engage. A playwright should be able to critically analyse the more theoretical aspects of, for example, Brechtian 'epic' theatre or Ibsen's naturalism, movements such as Theatre of the Absurd or 'In Yer Face' – and then use this critical analysis creatively for their own work. Of course, these are terms that probably mean very little to you at the moment, and they will be explored throughout the book, but as an example of critical thinking, remember that very often terms such as these have been applied retrospectively to groups of artists working around the same time and on similar themes or forms, who perhaps would never have seen themselves as part of a movement. These groups are given a name because they represent or highlight a creative zeitgeist of a particular era, but other work will have been created outside of these movements, and it is important for a playwright to always dig a little deeper in their research. This is the critical engagement I am aiming to encourage with this book, an understanding of theatre history, theatre movements and theatre that is happening in the world now that can lead to more nuanced, deeper research when creating your own plays.

What is writing for theatre?

Firstly, let's consider what the term *theatrical* might mean. If someone tells you that your script is not for the theatre or is not theatrical at all, what can you as the new writer take from that? To answer, it is useful to determine what it is that makes writing for theatre different.

Theatre happens in the now. One group of people, the audience, watch another group of people, the performers, act out a story in front of them. It is live, it is happening over a certain period of time, at a certain time, at a certain place and it is a shared experience for everyone in that room, both performers and audience.

Theatre writing is different to any other type of writing, just as screen-writing, writing for radio, for digital games, poetry, novel writing and short story writing are all different to any other type of writing. I am not making a case for any special treatment for playwriting, I am simply making a very basic statement. So whilst there may be some areas I explore in this book that work well for fiction writing or other types of script writing, I will always come back to the same principle: theatre happens live, in the here and now, and in a collaborative way. Acknowledging and then working within these constraints, and even seeing them as freeing for the imagination, is what makes a script theatrical.

The term 'new writing' also has a slightly more complicated relationship to theatre than it does to other media, especially other dramatic forms. For example, whilst we all may enjoy the odd TV repeat, or watching an old favourite movie, we will usually actively seek out new releases or new series of our favourite type of TV show. However, a theatre audience is often much more wary about paying to see a new piece of theatre, perhaps because in theatre the audience member has to be an active part of the show, and this means a certain amount of discomfort or hesitation before we even begin. This can be managed if we are going to see something very light hearted or something we know well, but it can be heightened if we are going to see something we might not 'get' or think is too 'arty'. In practice, this can mean that whilst there might be a range of new writing projects or initiatives, the-atres will often programme the firm favourites, the comedies, Shakespeare plays and musicals, because they know they can get an audience. There are a few theatres which are committed to new writing, such as The Bush and The Royal Court in London, but many provincial theatres may only produce one or two new plays a year, which means that paid work for the playwright can be hard to find if you are not open to new and creatively exciting ways of working, something that I will consider further in Part 2 of the book.

It could be argued that experiencing theatre has more in common with a gig or going to a football match than reading a novel or watching a film. It pulls on your emotions, it forces you to share that experience with 50, 500 or even 5,000 other people in the room with you, and after that particular show, there will never be the same performance again. What you are watch-ing live, right now, is unique. That is the beauty of theatre, it is ephemeral, immediate, and that aspect can make it a very emotional experience in a variety of ways. The script that you choose to write for theatre has to be theatrical in the truest sense of the word, by which I mean it must be a story that cannot be told in any other format than theatre. This live aspect makes critically studying writing for theatre quite tricky. All the student has from past plays or productions is the printed play script, perhaps the odd video clip or maybe some reviews or interviews with the playwright. These are all useful, but *seeing* as much theatre as you can will be as important as your reading.

So because I am focussing on new writing for theatre, I am not going to refer to hundreds and hundreds of plays you have never heard of, or if you have heard of them it is only because you 'did' writers such as Shakespeare or Arthur Miller at school.[2] Not that there is anything wrong with writers like Shakespeare or Arthur Miller, far from it, their plays are still being produced and you can learn a lot from seeing these productions. But, in my experience of teaching students new to theatre writing, this can be one of the most off-putting aspects of many of the craft books on our recommended reading lists. Students often tell me that referencing lots of 'old' plays with an assumption that the reader must know what the author is talking about makes them feel inadequate and stupid, and so turns them off theatre because it seems more 'intellectual' than screenwriting or novel writing. This is not an opinion I agree with, although I can understand the point that is being made. To help you, the emerging playwright, get to grips with the vast range of theatre work out there, there is a should-read list of plays at the back of this book. Many of the interviewees also refer to particular plays and, more importantly, you will notice, particular productions. All of this should act as a springboard from which you can find your own way through this huge history of theatre, published playscripts, craft texts and productions. Not all the answers are in this book, that would be far beyond the scope of one book, but my hope is that it will prompt you to ask questions, from which you can independently explore and research further.

There are some people mentioned by the interviewees that even I have never heard of (and I already consider myself a theatre geek!) but do not let this put you off writing for theatre. Simply do an Internet search to find out who they are and where you can find their work and then make up your own mind.

Another common problem I often come across amongst new writers is their belief that they should not read other work in case they are unduly influenced, or because they simply wish to create their own work and have

---

[2] Although of course you can go and explore all the plays in the 'should read' list at the back of this book!

no interest in the work of others. This is a flawed argument: to truly participate in any of the creative writing media, a writer has to understand that world, know who has written what, what has gone before, what is happening now and engage with the debates and creative explorations that are happening. The time of the isolated author writing furiously away up in their garret has long gone, if indeed it ever existed, so please expel that image from your mind, then you can begin to work properly as a writer.

On a practical note

One of the first questions I invariably get asked by students involves extreme concern about how to lay out a theatre script. It may seem strange that this comes up so early, often when a new writer knows little else about theatre writing, but I can understand it because theatre scripts do look different on the page when compared to prose and even scripts for other media. I usually advise students to look at other play scripts and see how they are laid out, because in truth, layout does not matter as much in theatre as it does in radio, TV or film. Layout needs to be clear, in a fairly plain font, and either 1.5 or double-spaced, but that is as far as the rules go really. If you look at other scripts you will see that many playwrights have their own way of laying out the script, so for ease, I can show you how I lay out mine:

Scene 1

We are in Sophia's bedroom, there is a large double bed and a huge dressing table. As the lights come up, Sophia brushes her hair. After a few seconds Marta walks in.

Marta   Is that it?
Sophia   One hundred.
Marta   Christ. (Beat) Do I have to wait?
Sophia   (Pause) Stop talking please.

The stage directions are different from the dialogue because they are in italics and go fully across the page. There is space between the character names and the dialogue line and directions to the actors on how to say a line or when to leave a beat or a pause, which I believe should always be used sparingly, are in brackets just before the dialogue. But look through any published or unpublished script and you will see lots of different layouts. Use whichever you feel comfortable with and which you feel represents your story, character and form of theatre in the best way. There are also plenty of softwares out there, often free, that help you with layout, but I would suggest you do not use a radio or screenplay layout for a theatre play, as these are immediately recognisable and whoever you send your script to may think that you are sending them a screenplay and not a theatre play at all, simply by the layout, which would be frowned upon in many literary departments. However, before you begin to create your first script, there is preparation that needs to be done to help you get into the mind-set of being a playwright, and that preparation might start with how to use this book.

Using this book

As you may have already gathered, this book assumes that the reader has little or no knowledge of theatre or of writing for theatre but is a creative writing student in some form. However, that is not to say that there will not be useful sections for those who may be further along in their playwriting career. The core aim of this book is to give a basic introduction to what writing for theatre means on all levels, creative, craft and critical.

The chapters are fairly self-contained; if, for example, you have a theatre history A-level, then please do feel free to skip the first two chapters. If you do not, then please read the first two chapters as it will give you a *very* basic grounding in what I will be talking about throughout the rest of the book.

There are two parts to this book: Foundations and Speculations.

Part 1 – Foundations

Theatre or drama has a long history, the longest history of any form of writing, and so we will start with a history of theatre to give you an understanding of how the tradition of Western, and particularly British, theatre making has evolved. I will then move on to some practical aspects of writing and making theatre, what traits and practices you need to be a playwright and end with some useful exercises as you prepare to write your first play.

Chapter 1 gives you a very brief history of theatre, from the Ancient Greeks to the twentieth century. It is important that as new writers you understand theatre history so that you know what has gone before you; even though the theatre you create will be new, live and will happen in the now, understanding what has gone before means you can work with or even against the traditions of theatre. This short chapter covers most of the main movements in theatre history, specifically British theatre, and if it fascinates you, I would encourage you to read more; if it does not, at least it will give you a basic grounding to move on from.

Chapter 2 looks at the cultures and debates surrounding theatre by thinking about some of the great theatre innovators of the past up to the end of the twentieth century. The term innovator can be a controversial one, but in this chapter I asked the interviewees to talk about writers who they believe fundamentally changed certain aspects of what it means to make theatre. More experienced theatre makers may agree or disagree with the list, but again I hope it will act as a springboard for further exploration. One of the most important aspects of understanding the cultures of theatre is contextualising them; theatre moves forward constantly and therefore each new movement speaks to and builds on those of the past.

Chapter 3 is about establishing practice. It looks at why we write for theatre, how to write for theatre and how those I interviewed came to work in theatre in the first place. Theatre is often seen as something of an elitist arena, where only clever people who understand Shakespeare can work, but this could not be farther from the truth, and hopefully some of the very personal stories from theatre makers will highlight how very egalitarian theatre can be.

Chapter 4 explores the qualities needed to be a playwright. Interviewees suggest certain traits inherent or necessary to be a good playwright as well as how and why these qualities work. Being any type of writer is not simply about being able to think up a good story and being able to type that story up – it is about being disciplined in your work ethic and understanding which craft techniques and which aspects of your own personality you need to work on. This may seem like a strange area to explore, but writing is inherently personal. Every writer works in a different way, has their own process, but having guidance from those already out there doing it will help and I hope inspire new playwrights.

Chapter 5 explores the building blocks of playwriting, including form and structure, story and subject, character and dialogue. As I mentioned above, this is not as such a 'how-to' book in terms of these more technical or craft aspects, but it is a 'how-to' book in that the main aim is to help show the aspiring playwright how to be a playwright. Therefore, I will explore these craft elements but in terms of what they mean for the stage, assuming that as a student of creative writing you will have some knowledge of the basics of these craft terms already.

Chapter 6 sums up the key points in Part 1 through a series of exercises that explore some of the ideas discussed up to this point, as well as exploring the different shapes a theatre space can be.

Part 2 – Speculations

The second part of this book, Speculations, thinks about different ways of making theatre and also where theatre may go in the future. We are currently in what is being called the digital age, and theatre is a very analogue art form, so this part explores different ways of working as well as considering how relevant theatre is today. Of course, it has to be acknowledged that the cultural landscape changes constantly, so this part explores speculatively in a more personally creative way, to ensure that it remains relevant for as long as possible. But hopefully there are some useful practical tips too.

Chapter 7 explores the current and future possibilities for writing theatre; it discusses current cultures and debates of theatre in the 'digital age' and considers whether or not we still even need theatre, and if we do, what sort of world new playwrights might be entering. This chapter also examines what types of theatre are out there in terms of commercial, subsidised and fringe theatre, as well as development potential for new writers.

Chapter 8 examines some of the new innovators of the present and potentially of the future. Interviewees discuss those who they think are currently creating exciting new work and those who are on the cusp of being exciting creative innovators of performance work, and who emerging playwrights can learn from.

Chapter 9 discusses how we may change or explore established practice in theatre writing. It considers what writers find inspirational in theatre, as well as forms of theatre such as ethnographic, verbatim and participant-led, and the role of the dramaturg in current theatre practice.

Chapter 10 thinks about new voices and new forms of theatre, exploring different ways of collaborating, how to get your own work in front of an audience and using different art forms in theatre.

Chapter 11 sums up the key points from Part 2 and also provides some speculative exercises to try and help new writers think beyond the usual type of theatre writing. There is also a list of companies and organisations playwrights should know about, which although not exhaustive, is a good starting point. Finally, there is the 'should-read' play list for you to explore either on the page or, if you can, in performance, along with a selection of craft and critical texts.

A collaborative approach to writing about playwriting

As I have already noted, theatre is by its very nature collaborative, and because of this I want this book to create a sense of collaboration or discussion. So, whilst I am writing the main body of the book, other writers, directors, dramaturgs and literary managers have contributed, enabling me to give you a more rounded view of what making new theatre is like in these early decades of the twenty-first century. These are people making theatre now. Some might be on their way to becoming grandees of the theatre, some may always work quietly in the background encouraging other writers and theatre makers, and some, if they are not already counted as such, may be on the brink of becoming superstars. But all of these people make and facilitate good theatre, and that is why I wanted to bring them together to discuss what writing for theatre is, what it means, why we do it and how we can continue to do it when, to some, theatre seems anachronistic in this digital age. The input from these theatre makers is invaluable in creating critical links, supporting arguments and exploring the realities of writing for theatre in the twenty-first century. There may be contradictions, there may be no one clear line you can follow to write your first play, but that is simply a reflection of theatre. That is how theatre works. Discussion and debate, even arguments, are all part of the way we create, and are therefore all part of this book.

The interviewees are (with their jobs or roles at the time of interview):

Suzanne Bell: Dramaturg and New Writing Associate at the Royal Exchange Theatre, Manchester. Suzanne originally trained as a director and worked previously at the Everyman Theatre in Liverpool as dramaturg and literary manager from 2001 before joining the Royal Exchange in 2012.

Ella Carmen Greenhill: a playwright (on attachment at Paines Plough) known for plays such as *Plastic Figurines* (Box of Tricks), *Made in Britain* (The Old Red Lion), *Beethoven's Always Right* (Theatre 503) and also co-runs Pimento Theatre with Joe Ward Munrow.

Billy Cowan: a playwright and creative writing lecturer at Edge Hill University. He is one of the directors for Truant Theatre Company and is known for plays such as *Smilin' Through* (Finborough Theatre, Birmingham Rep and Contact, Manchester), *Transitions* which won the International Playwriting Award in 2010, and his most recent plays, both of which toured the UK, *The Right Ballerina* and *Still Ill.*

Rob Drummer: associate dramaturg at The Bush Theatre and an associate at Company of Angels. Previous work includes principal dramaturg and literary manager for the High Tide Festival Theatre and he has developed plays for companies such as Soho Theatre, Watford Palace and the Edinburgh Festival.

Kevin Dyer: a playwright who is an associate artist with Action Transport Theatre and The Dukes in Lancaster, and has been commissioned for over 50 plays, having most recently come back from Canada working on a play called *The Minotaur.* He has also directed plays and written for radio.

Fin Kennedy: a playwright and a director of Tamasha Theatre Company, as well as the creator of Schoolwrights (a scheme where playwrights work in schools to create new work) and the In Battalions Delphi Study into funding for British theatre. He is multi-award winning, having won awards for the plays *How To Disappear Completely And Never Be Found, Locked In* and *The Unravelling*.

Ruth Little: a dramaturg, writer and associate director of Cape Farewell, who has worked with companies such as Sadler's Wells, the Akram Khan company and was literary manager at Out of Joint theatre company, Soho Theatre, The Young Vic and The Royal Court.

Steven Luckie: associate director at Birmingham Rep, has worked across the country as a freelance director and is known for plays such as *Talking About Men* which had a regional tour after its London run.

Joe Ward Munrow: a playwright (on attachment at the Everyman, Liverpool) who is known for *Held* at the Everyman and is co-director of Pimento Theatre with Ella Carmen Greenhill, whose most recent production was *Mind The Gap*. Joe also teaches playwriting at universities and writing programmes across the North West.

Elizabeth Newman: associate director at The Octagon Theatre in Bolton[3] where she has worked since 2010. She is responsible for the new writing programme at The Octagon, and previous work included numerous freelance productions. She has also been associate artist at Southwark Playhouse.

Lizzie Nunnery: a playwright (formerly writer in residence at the Everyman, Liverpool) who is best known for the plays *The Swallowing Dark* and *Intemperance* amongst many others. She also performs in a folk duo with Vidar Norheim and teaches playwriting at a number of universities and writing programmes in the North West.

Adam Quayle: co-director of Box of Tricks Theatre, a North West based theatre company, who have produced plays such as *In Doggerland*, the *Word:Play* series, *The Other Team* and *Plastic Figurines*.

Holly Race Roughan: a freelance director who has worked at The Royal Exchange in Manchester (*Pages From My Songbook, Skylines* amongst others), the Young Vic, Theatre 503 and Southwark Playhouse.

---

[3] In March 2015 Newman became artistic director of The Octagon, Bolton.

Joe Sumsion: artistic director of The Dukes, Lancaster where he has directed numerous productions. Previously, he was the artistic director of Action Transport Theatre as well as working as a freelance director.

Lawrence Till: a director for both theatre and TV (*Mr Selfridge, Shameless*) he has been artistic director at The Octagon, Bolton and the Watford Palace. Till also adapted *Kes* for the stage.

Chris Thorpe: a founder member of Unlimited Theatre and is an associate artist with Third Angel. He has written and/or created many productions, including *There Has Possibly Been An Incident, I Wish I Was Lonely, Oh F**k Moment* amongst many others.

Hannah Tyrrell-Pinder: co-director of Box of Tricks Theatre, a North West based theatre company who have produced plays such as *In Doggerland*, the *Word:Play* series, *The Other Team* and *Plastic Figurines*.

Zosia Wand: a playwright who writes for both theatre and radio; her works include *Quicksand* and *Hansel and Gretel* (both at The Dukes, Lancaster) and *Treehouse* for Radio 4.

All interviews took place in 2013.

Role definitions

Playwright – notice that this is written Play*wright* not Play*write* (although of course we refer to *playwriting* and not *playwrighting*, which always seems a bit of a shame to me, because playwrighting is such a great word!). The word *wright* is pretty much obsolete now, but it is interesting to note its origins and be aware that there is a sense of craft in this form of writing. Writing plays involves the shaping and crafting of the piece of theatre, just as a wheelwright or a shipwright shapes and crafts. In an interview quoted in Duska Radosavljevic's book, *Theatre Making: Interplay Between Text and Performance in the 21st Century* (2013), Simon Stephens, one of this century's most celebrated playwrights, says:

> Absolutely integral to my methodology of teaching was something that I think is in the intellectual metabolism of the Royal Court, which is a consideration of what makes a play. The Royal Court is a theatre which is built on the notions of 'plays being wrought rather than written.' (p. 203)

The craft of the playwright is here underlined as just as important as the imagination, and this is something I will continue to consider throughout the book.

Dramaturg – this is possibly the hardest definition to explain, because the role changes so much depending on where the dramaturg is situated. The role can be taken on by other playwrights, directors or literary managers, but a basic description is that a dramaturg works with the playwright on the words on the page, helping the playwright to shape the best possible play and the best possible audience experience that they can, enabling and facilitating collaborative work. I explore the terms dramaturg and dramaturgy a little more in Part 2.

Director – this is the person who interprets the written text with the actors, who asks questions of the playwright, who shares the responsibility of making this piece of theatre work on stage. In *The Cambridge Introduction to Modern British Theatre* (2009), Simon Shepherd suggests that 'the concept of the theatre director was only just beginning to emerge at the start of the twentieth century' in the UK (p. 102), and this was more of an American term, however most theatre productions are now led by a director. Producing theatres are often run by an artistic director, who will both curate or programme the season of plays, creatively running the building, and direct some of the productions.

Literary Associates/Managers or New Writing Associates – theatres who are funded through public monies (Arts Council England for example) often have a remit to encourage new writing and this can be done in a variety of ways – through workshops, competitions or building relationships with writers, for example. This is most often the job of the literary associate, literary manager or new writing associate.

These roles will be mentioned throughout the book, but, as Elizabeth Newman noted, many people who create theatre often prefer the term 'theatre-maker' because there are a number of potential cross-overs with some of these creative theatre roles – for example, you may be a writer who directs or a writer who is also a dramaturg. What must be remembered though is that everyone is working towards the same goal – making a good piece of theatre.

There are also a number of other jobs in theatre that it is useful to know about at this early stage, and they are:

Actors – the people who will work with the director to bring the characters and the story alive for the audience.

Designer – this might be one person or a team of people, but the costumes and the set will be designed and made (through a Wardrobe department and a Construction, Carpentry or Workshop department) for a particular production.

Lighting Designer/Sound Designer – depending on the production, there may be a sound designer, but there will almost always be a lighting designer working with the Electricians or LX Department.

Stage Management – this team of people cover a wide range of jobs, from running 'the book' in rehearsals to finding props and furniture (although some bigger theatre companies might also have a Props department as part of the design team or as part of the Workshop). They will also cover all the actual performances, complete scene changes and ensure the smooth working of the show.

Marketing – this can be a freelance person producing a few leaflets and a website or a full department covering press, front of house and box office. These people will sell your show to your audience.

This is a very basic list but goes some way to showing how collaborative making a piece of theatre is, and how many people are involved in any production – from the smallest fringe show to the largest commercial musical – although of course in some smaller productions one person might take on several of these roles. Whilst it should never act as a stopper to your creativity, it is useful for any playwright to keep in mind the number of people that need to be involved for a play to be performed or produced – and all these people will have to believe in your script, a situation which can be as exciting as it is scary.

Part I

Foundations

1 A Brief History of Theatre for Playwrights

Writing for theatre means being in the now, in the present, because theatre is in its very essence ephemeral. A performance happens live, at a particular time with a particular audience, and it will never happen that way again. Of course it can be recorded, filmed, written down and published, but part of the experience of live drama, the one thing that makes it different to all other forms of storytelling, is the shared experience of the audience linked to a particular performance – and that can never be recorded, at least not with current technology. In its story, theme and form, a new play will inevitably reflect the world around the playwright at the time of writing.

Fin Kennedy: Out of all the art forms I think theatre lives most in the present tense, and possibly a bit in the immediate future. Theatre is about how we live now and you experience it now. And I'm sure there's the equivalent in theatre history of when Dylan picked up his electric guitar,[1] but it doesn't really interest me. I'm glad we've moved away from drawing room drama. I'm glad we started to look to Europe a little bit more. But I couldn't point to a timeline and say it is this, this and this, because I don't really think about theatre in that way – I tell the best story I can tell, in the best way I know how, in the moment I tell it. And I go to see theatre as an audience member in the same way. I very rarely go to see a classic or a dead writer or set in the past, and I'm not interested in museum theatre in that way. And yes, I know there are classics that can talk to us now, you can do *Henry V* and make it about Iraq or whatever, but the question I always have to ask is: is that better than commissioning a play about that subject set in the present day? There is a preponderance of revivals of classics because of our director-led profession, and it gives directors a chance to kind of show-off – directors hate it when I say that, I always get into arguments with them – but theatre is about how we live now.

---

[1] In 1965 Bob Dylan, known as an acoustic folk artist, decided to use an amplified band to much controversy at the time!

So if a playwright is working in the now, why am I starting with a brief history of theatre? Why is this important to the emerging theatre geek? Simply because this is what it means to be a geek. It means knowing as much as you can about your subject. It means critically evaluating your subject, and it means applying that knowledge appropriately.

> **Ruth Little:** In the West we've inherited a canon and a tradition and it's up to us to continually reassess the current capacity of those 'big' plays – the 'classics' – to inform and inspire us in relation to our own lives. But we also have a responsibility to the unheard voices – the plays that were disregarded or suppressed in their own time, the overlooked gestures that can create a more diverse and complex sense of our own histories and anxieties. Woyzeck, Ubu, *A Raisin in the Sun*; I hope I would have felt their significance and power at the time. Or at the first performance of Stravinsky's *Rite of Spring*, when audience and artists colluded to create a theatrical event out of Stravinsky and Nijinsky's pioneering collaboration. Interestingly for me it's the 'ugly' work that has made the difference, because it breaks the pattern, creates a new aesthetic, hurts. *Blasted* by Sarah Kane mattered for the same reason. None of these plays set out to be ugly or challenging for its own sake – they actively and passionately provoked, with all the tools at their disposal. That was their gesture – the rest of us gave them their status over time.

There is the old saying that history is written by the victors. If that is the case, why should those of us who are creating theatre in the now take any notice of historic work? Why should we take notice of a few writers and directors, considered to be great in the opinion of a few academics or theatre makers who might be giving them more status than they actually had when they were working in the now? There are many arguments for and against the literary canon, which I won't be going into here, but in reality looking at theatre history is not necessarily the same as looking at canonical texts that have been handed down to us by dead white men who deemed themselves taste makers. There are in fact a couple of reasons why understanding theatre through its history is important for a playwright.

The first reason is that same ephemeral nature already mentioned. Whilst it suggests that theatre happens in the moment and then is lost, theatre can't help but be secured in its own history. Many books on making theatre will refer to historic examples simply because this is all that is recorded; we can only attempt to know through published scripts, critical reviews and explorations into the ways theatre has developed over the ages, whilst always being aware that we can never experience it in the same way as those contemporary audiences. Film, TV and radio plays can all be reviewed, re-watched and re-experienced, as can novels, short stories and poetry collections. Theatre in its performance form cannot, which is part of what makes writing and creating theatre so exhilarating. Talk to theatre makers about that buzz from an audience laughing, crying or concentrating on their piece whilst in the same space as them, and you will see that glassy look come into their eyes as they search for words about how brilliant, terrifying and exciting that can be. But no writer or theatre maker can be unaware of what has gone before, of where they fit within the tradition of creating theatre for this very reason: the ephemeral nature of theatre means we have to root ourselves in our history; we have to be aware of what has gone before so that we can understand what is happening in the now and what can possibly happen in the future.

The second reason comes back to that concept of geekiness. Theatre makers like to know and understand what has gone before. This might be for a variety of reasons, such as subverting genres or forms of theatre, learning what has worked for centuries and not re-inventing the wheel – or specifically re-inventing the wheel because it needs re-inventing to stop us all getting bored – and learning from grandees, past and present. We want to feel connected, be part of that history and understand the very essence of theatre making. This is why we write theatre; it can create emotions and reactions that are tangible to us in the here and now, whilst learning from, and perhaps even referencing, what has gone before us. And because theatre is collaborative there is a sense of a community of theatre makers that we belong to, and knowing our history can add to that sense of belonging.

There are some excellent books on the history of theatre (see the further reading section at the back of the book for some of these); so what follows is a very brief history, certainly not in any way definitive, that situates drama as the oldest form of storytelling and explains within a linear timeline what some of those important moments in history were. It is of necessity brief, and will concentrate mostly on Western theatre, again for reasons of space but also because you can explore some of the more exciting areas of Japanese, Asian or African theatre once you've grasped what being a theatre geek is all about! The assumption here is that you are a writer aiming to work primarily in the UK, certainly writing in the English language, and it therefore makes most sense to concentrate on this area of theatre history for your basic introduction.

Ancient theatre

As Elizabeth Newman points out, humans have told and enjoyed stories with a beginning, middle and end, where people are at the heart of an adventure, from the very start of civilisation; what are termed 'cave paintings' tell a basic story:

> **Elizabeth Newman:** There was a man, he fought a beast, he killed the beast, he took the beast home for food. Man, in danger, wins, happy ever after. Storytelling relates to life, how we experience existence, which is why theatre uses sound and seeing, because it is how we experience life.

Humans telling each other stories, drama in other words, is recorded as starting with the Ancient Greeks. However there is evidence from around the world that drama came through religious ritual, movements and chanting, or perhaps songs and dances, that formed part of god worship and ritual. Hartnoll (1985) suggests that

> The origin of the modern theatre can be found in the dithyramb (or unison hymn) sung round the altar of Dionysus [...] by a chorus of fifty men, five from each of the ten tribes of Attica. (p. 8)

This is theatre in terms of form, not necessarily storytelling, and it is interesting to note that for centuries entertainment and religion or ritual were closely tied, that the coming together of the community to share experience had both spiritual and entertainment value. We may have lost a sense of that spiritual value gained from theatre being linked to organised religion, but there is still a sense of catharsis that links to the spiritual, as I shall go on to explore below.

Over time, this form of worship began to include tales of the gods, acted out by members of the dithyramb chorus. The legend is that one such chorus member, Thespis, moved out of the chorus during one ritual to begin to tell the story, crucially 'acting' as one of the characters.[2] The audience, or congregation, enjoyed this storytelling and, true to the maxim of always giving an audience what they want, this became part of the ritual. Over time, the Greeks began to produce playwrights who would craft stories well-known to the citizens into entertainment, still linked to religious festivals, as indeed were the Olympics, and a type of theatre festival or competition began. There were three types of play: Satyr, Tragedies and Comedies.

---

[2] Leading to the term 'Thespians' often used to describe actors (although not always in the most respectful tone nowadays).

We know very little about Satyr plays today. They may have been light relief or they may have been dumbshows, but they almost certainly involved creatures who were strange half-animal half-human creations. We do, however, have work extant from three writers of Tragedy and two of Comedy.

Aeschylus (born circa 525 BC) was the creator of the only surviving tragic trilogy, *The Oresteia*, which covers the murder of a king by his wife and her lover, the revenge of his son, Orestes, who kills his mother, and is then persecuted for matricide. Aeschylus probably wrote over 90 plays, of which only a handful survive, but he is known for his poetic style and exploration of what is often termed 'cosmic' themes. Technically, he is also credited with introducing a second actor to the storytelling troupe of actor and chorus; by this point, the chorus in these plays often acted as narrator or questioner and would explain time passing or the backstory.

Sophocles (born circa 496 BC) was the writer of the Oedipus plays, and was credited with introducing actor number three. He also wrote about 90 plays and was more concerned with the human lives of men and women rather than the 'cosmic' lives of the gods.

Finally, Euripides (born circa 485 BC) completes this trio of Ancient Greek writers of tragedy. Born around 11 years after Sophocles, his body of work was similar in size, and we have about 18 of his plays extant, including *Medea* and *The Trojan Women*.

The two best-known comic writers are Aristophanes (born circa 448 BC) and Menander (circa 342 BC).

Aristophanes is known mostly for his plays *Wasps*, *Clouds* and *Frogs*, and it is thought he wrote around 40 plays in all. Comic writing allowed for satire, slapstick and bawdiness and was obviously a form of light relief for the audience, but in the form of satire it was also used to criticise the state. Menander, born over a century later, brought in a lighter form of comedy, much less offensive on all counts, of which we have about five examples.

The Tragedies cover the lives of the gods, coming from the myths and legends of Homer's time, and focus on a great hero who usually faces a fate often worse than death. Performed at religious festivals (often for prizes or awards, showing how highly the writers were valued in their society at the time), these plays induced in the audience what is known as *catharsis*. This is quite a difficult emotion to describe, but it links closely to how modern audiences can feel watching a great play, and is therefore worth some examination.

Catharsis is often thought to be a purging or purification of emotions, but I think of it more as a release of emotions that mirror those of the hero in his downfall through empathy with his situation. There is also a sense of thankfulness and relief that the audience members do not have to go through this situation themselves, ending in a type of emotional exhaustion. This sounds awful and a lot to expect an audience to go through, but think about the last time you watched a really emotional film, where the hero or heroine battles valiantly but ultimately fails, or the relief when they emerge triumphant. That sense of having a heightened emotional state is the reason we as humans watch these stories; we want that involvement, we want to experience lives other than our own, and catharsis is part of that process.

Ancient Greek theatre also set up particular practical tropes, some of which we would still recognise today. Actors wore costumes that clearly defined what type of character they were, and these costumes were supplemented by masks which also clearly defined the character and made them visible to all of the often vast audience. Also, because there were at most three actors but more than three speaking parts, it meant that actors could perform as one character, go off for a quick change and come on as another, showing their versatility and talent.

The temples changed into theatre spaces, with a circular stage area called the *orchestra* for the chorus and a raised stage area behind this for the actors with a wooden construction known as a *skene* (where we get our word 'scene' from) which was a type of low building housing various devices that the Greeks employed for special effects. The skene could also be painted as a backdrop. Ancient theatre was a time of invention and change, a time of what Chris Thorpe terms 'pivotal moments'.

> **Chris Thorpe:** I was reading recently of the origin of Deus Ex Machina, it being a plot device of the god who comes down and sorts everything out, referencing the fact that the actors who played gods were winched down onto the stage with an actual machine, and I guess that must have been a defining moment in theatre when it happened, that seeded a lot of things – not that the idea of Deus Ex Machina is a useful or a brilliant idea for theatre now, but these pivotal moments, that maybe you're not even aware of, as I wasn't aware of that, have given rise, because they worked, they subverted those conventions – those are the pivotal moments. The first time someone represented the death of a human being on stage. The first time someone represented a living politician on stage. The first time someone took words that had actually been spoken and put them on stage. The first time someone played film as part of a performance on stage. You can imagine pivotal moments in all of those ways.

And this is exactly why an understanding of the history of theatre matters. It is about finding those pivotal moments for yourself as a playwright, placing yourself in your moment in its history and using these pivotal moments to inform or change, or even help you create your own pivotal moments, thinking critically about what those moments meant in their own context and then using that understanding creatively through your writing.

It is clear to see how trends came and went – the tragedians were all active, and popular, years before the comic writers, whose work became perhaps more audience-friendly as time went on. But it is not only from vase paintings, scraps of plays, the odd complete play and the remains of theatres in Delphi or Epidaurus that we know about Greek theatre.

> **Suzanne Bell:** If we really think back to: what is theatre? It is someone telling a story in front of a campfire to a group of people. If the story isn't good enough, that person is either going to get told to shut up or they're going to get pelted with rocks or people are just going to walk away from the campfire, and I think we forget about this sometimes. We forget that theatre is about communicating a story and why you want to communicate that story live, how you take that audience on a journey, how you tell that story – because it is still a story, it is still that campfire moment.

> Sophocles, Euripides, Aristophanes and the Greeks [playwrights] then subsequently Aristotle and Plato's writings, are still hugely influential. *The Iliad* came from an oral history, a storytelling tradition, so it was still like theatre, which makes it for me a defining historical moment.

One of the most enduring staples of theatre history is the section in Aristotle's work *Poetics* where he talks about the three Unities. It may seem preposterous that over 2,500 years later we in theatre are still talking about some Ancient Greek bloke called Aristotle, but the fact remains that as a starting point for a writer new to theatre, the Unities are perhaps the best place.

So, what are these 'Unities'? They are known as the Unity of Time, the Unity of Place and the Unity of Action. Many people who work in theatre and talk about the Unities perhaps have never read *Poetics*, perhaps have not even realised that they have not read *Poetics*, simply because it is something that is spoken about so often. What does it mean though? It means exactly what I have already been talking about in the Introduction and start of this chapter, namely, the live experience of storytelling happening now. For example, on TV or in a film you can have many short scenes, often with little to no dialogue, that flash back or forwards in time and have a number of locations. This is much more difficult to achieve in theatre, and the fact that film technology freed the artist from the constraints of the Unities is, I think, telling in that the Unities can be seen as both a constraint as well as a useful creative tool.

On a very basic level, Aristotle is telling the theatre maker that to make good tragedy it has to take place mostly in the one location, it has to run in a linear fashion time wise and that there must be a sense of the action building. Many Ancient Greek tragedies, therefore, often 'tell' rather than 'show' a lot of backstory, because the audience comes in at the crucial moment, when the final fall of the hero is imminent. David Edgar in *How Plays Work* (2009, pp. 29–30) uses Sophocles's *Oedipus* to highlight this, because the play starts two-thirds of the way through the actual story, which is narrated as the backstory that explains the reasons why plagues and famines are now decimating Thebes. So whilst at this stage there are three actors and a chorus on stage enacting the drama, the performance is still not that far away from the Homeric form of oral storytelling, as only a portion of the story is happening in the 'now'. This is useful for new playwrights to think about, because many of the craft texts, or 'how-to' books, on writing for theatre will talk about the careful handling of exposition and the directive to 'show not tell'.[3] Having an understanding of the origins of drama as live storytelling along a timeline can help the new playwright move away from this 'telling' style, or help the writer to re-imagine how this telling might work for a modern audience. For example, I could argue that Tim Crouch's *The Author* (2009) revisits this type of storytelling feature, and although it plays with form, the actors discuss events that have happened in the past that have brought them to this point.

Ancient Greece sets the basic groundwork for creating theatre for an audience as live event-storytelling. When the Roman Empire came along, conquering Greece and spreading across the globe, it took many of its ideas about theatre from the Greeks, often using and expanding the same stories and myths.

The two Roman writers we know the most about are Plautus (born 254 BC) and Terence (born circa 195 BC), a freed slave who wrote six plays in total. Examples of their work do exist and both were comic dramatists, but it would be fair to say that whilst the Romans built theatre spaces across the empire, and by doing so, instilled the idea of communal storytelling in a dramatic form into many new cultures, much of the innovation in storytelling or theatricality came from their Greek predecessors. As Rome expanded its empire, Roman theatre descended into spectacle, flooding arenas and enacting full sea battles, for example, or having an emphasis on bikini-clad dancing girls rather than 'catharsis' and story. But it did introduce the rest

---

[3] Exposition is the backstory of the plot that the audience need to know to understand what is happening on stage now.

of its empire to that idea of the communal theatrical space and the entertainment value of theatre, laying the foundations for many different forms
to come.

Medieval theatre

Following the fall of the Roman Empire, the next major point in Western
theatre history to consider comes during the middle ages and medieval
times.

British medieval theatre (roughly fifth–fifteenth century) can be split into
two main areas: theatre linked to the Church through Passion plays, and
the court theatre troupe entertaining the wealthy through ballads and pag-
eants. Both involved visual storytelling to an audience but for very different
reasons.

The Church held a very strong position in medieval society across
Europe, with the services intoned in Latin, which the common populace
could rarely understand. The congregation were mostly illiterate and unable to read the bible or holy books for themselves. So what are known as
'liturgical plays', often performed and written by priests, to tell the stories
from the bible, came into being to help the congregation understand what
was being preached in the services. Eventually these plays moved out of the
Church and became known as Passion plays if they concentrated on the
life and death of Christ or Mystery plays if they were about other aspects of
Christian life. If it seems that this historic moment in time is too long ago
to have any relevance today, you only have to think about the school nativity play or the recent famous Passion plays such as Michael Sheen's *Port
Talbot Passion* (2011), the *Manchester Passion* (2006) and the Chester
Mystery Plays, which still happen with a community cast every year.

The court troupe was more involved in pure entertainment through acrobatics, comedy and music. What was important about the development
of the court troupe was the aristocratic patronage of art and entertainment that was established during this time, which would go on to include
theatre troupes during the Renaissance. However, whilst understanding
this moment in theatre history is important, there was very little innovation
as far as playwrights were concerned because, unlike the liturgical plays,
they were created for entertainment, not for religious reasons, and as such
very few survive to the present day. They were practical rather than creative
endeavours.

The liturgical play moved on to become the morality play, such as the
anonymously written *Everyman* which concentrated less on the biblical

stories and more on the moral issues of living contemporary life for ordinary men and women. But this late medieval/early Tudor period overlapped with the new creative moment that began in Italy.

The Renaissance

The Renaissance (roughly fourteenth to seventeenth century) may have started in Italy but it moved throughout Europe relatively quickly. The movement was characterised by a return to the Ancient Greek and Roman classics in literature, theatre and art. This again may still seem like an awful long time ago, but as Zosia Wand points out, this period still has a lot of relevance for modern writers:

> **Zosia Wand:** An important time to think about is the Renaissance Theatre, Shakespeare and Marlowe. What interests me about that time is that the role of the audience seemed much more important. Having to entertain and engage that audience was crucial and I think sometimes nowadays theatre loses that. Sometimes it seems as if the audience is not very important at all, and that's when it doesn't work very well. I like the fact that during the Renaissance people stood very close to the stage, they didn't sit. I think it is fantastic that some of these old theatres have been revived, like Stratford and The Globe; they are incredible places to go and see how it all started out.
>
> For me the key thing is that theatre started out as something for the masses, it was entertainment, but over time it became something exclusive and I dislike that intensely. I think when it is exclusive, it is not working, and there is something fundamentally wrong. It should appeal. Snobbery around theatre is unacceptable.

Communal entertainment for the masses saw a move away from the bear pit and cock fighting entertainments that were very popular at the time, to the telling of stories from other countries and other times but which still somehow managed to tell the audience something about their own country and their own time. As Wand suggests, because theatre opened up to the masses it was a very democratic form of entertainment; all classes could go to see one of these plays.

It was during the Renaissance that, through aristocratic patronage, the concept of theatre companies came about, leading to the idea that theatre could be a profession. So the Renaissance saw a move away from the

Church and back to an understanding of the ancient classics, with a return to the stories of men and women rather than of God and the saints, democratising entertainment across all classes.

Shakespeare, Webster, Jonson and Marlowe are perhaps now the best-known British Renaissance playwrights, but there were a great many writers during this time. As such, these writers looked back to the ancient classical times and the role of the playwright, or the poet as they were also known, ensuring that this role became recognised as creatively important once again. As poets, they often wrote in sonnet form, but in their plays their dialogue was often in iambic pentameter, rhyming couplets or blank verse. Nowadays, this can seem off-putting on the page, but the point is that there was a story being told through this use of poetic language, and by interrogating the texts you can often see how tightly structured these plays were. A really useful text to explore for this is *Backwards and Forwards* (1983) by David Ball, which gives the theatre maker a structured reading of *Hamlet*, setting up skills to analyse any play but also incredibly useful for redrafting your own play.

I feel I need to say very little on Shakespeare, and the interviewees do explore his importance in the next chapter, but perhaps some of the names of his contemporaries are less well known to you.

Christopher Marlowe (born 1564, the same year as Shakespeare) was quite a dashing and colourful figure. He was alleged to have been a spy and also an atheist, a very dangerous accusation at the time, and he died before he was thirty in mysterious circumstances. He wrote many plays, but best known amongst them are *Tamburlaine*, *The Jew of Malta* and *The Tragical History of Doctor Faustus*.

John Webster (born circa 1580) is best known for his tragedies based on Italian stories, which can often be quite dark, such as *The White Devil* and *The Duchess of Malfi*. He also collaborated on plays with other writers such as Thomas Dekker and Thomas Middleton.

Ben Jonson (b. 1572) was part of The Admiral's Men theatre company, and his first big success was *Every Man in His Humour*, which apparently had Shakespeare in the cast. He was known for his comic and satirical plays, often satirising other writers at first, before becoming more critical of the world around him as time went on, landing him with a brief spell in prison. He is known to have collaborated with the famous architect and theatre designer Inigo Jones. He went on to write *The Alchemist*, *Volpone* and *Bartholomew Fair* amongst many others.

This was an incredibly important time in British theatre, setting the groundwork for much of what was to come next.

The seventeenth century to the twentieth century

The Restoration

The next pivotal moment in British theatre history starts with the English Civil War (1642–1651) when the Puritan victors banned theatre, amongst other leisure pursuits, putting an end to the work Shakespeare and his contemporaries had begun, and in 1648 the Puritans ordered that many of the theatre buildings be demolished. It was not until the Restoration of the monarchy and the return of King Charles II in 1660 that theatres were also 'restored'. More opulent theatres were built and the king and the aristocracy enjoyed theatre as a leisure pursuit, consequently making it less democratic an entertainment and moving theatre into the preserve of the upper classes.

You may already be familiar with the term Restoration Comedies, leading on to eighteenth-century works such as Gay's *Beggar's Opera* (which Bertolt Brecht later used as a basis for his and Kurt Weil's *Threepenny Opera)* or Congreve's *The Way of the World*, but importantly this is a time when, as Elizabeth Newman points out, women were allowed to act female roles for the first time as well as write plays. In pretty much the whole of theatre history up to this point, only men had been allowed to act on stage, with boys taking female roles, and writing plays had not been seen as a potential career for a woman at all. Of course, history suggests that these new women actors and playwrights were not held in the highest repute, one of the most famous being the king's mistress, Nell Gwynne. However it was still a major step forward in theatre history, and it is almost impossible to imagine what the effect was on those writers who knew that from then on their female characters would be played by female actors.

Aphra Behn (b. 1640), is perhaps the best-known female playwright of this time, and she wrote plays such as *The Rover, The Forc'd Marriage* and *The Amorous Prince.* She also wrote the quite controversial novel *Oroonoko* which explores the story of an enslaved African prince, highlighting again how theatre writers have often used their writing to explore wider social and political questions.

Pantomime

It is also around this time that pantomime began to develop in England, although not perhaps in the way we understand it now. The roots of pantomime were in the Italian sixteenth-century form of the Commedia Dell'Arte tradition, which used mime, masks and stock characters such as Pantolone,

Pulcinella - who became our Punch - Scaramouche, Pierrot and Pierrette and Harlequin. The roots going back to the ancient Satyr and comic plays are clear here, and the influence on the courtly masques in England during the sixteenth and seventeenth centuries brought about the development of the Harlenquinade story during the seventeenth century. This story saw two young lovers escape the young woman's father, who pursues them with his comic clowns. These were silent 'dumbshows' with dancing and acrobatics, but during the nineteenth century there was a move away from this basic story into fairy tales. The famous clown Grimaldi also brought a slapstick humour to the pantomime, and the form became defined as a children's form of theatre, being shown mostly at Christmas because this was when the children were on holiday.

It is important to think about these more popular types of entertainment as well as the more text-based plays, because theatre making can borrow from all forms but comes back to the same classical routes: for example, ballet and opera flourished around this time in France and Italy, and here we can see how the links to modern-day musicals and rock operas come via European opera and ballet, which in turn can trace their roots all the way back to Greek Satyr plays and Roman extravaganzas.

The Actor–Manager

The eighteenth century saw the rise of the actor–manager, such as the famous David Garrick. This saw theatre become more commercial as it moved away from aristocratic patronage. The choice of which play to produce now became the preserve of the actor–manager, who often had an eye on the role he would play, rather than on the creative innovation for the playwright. What also hindered the creativity of playwrights was the introduction of censorship of new plays by the Lord Chamberlain, a practice that was not abolished until 1968, so that it was often easier to stay with the tried-and-tested 'classics' from the Renaissance (often with a few rewrites to suit the actor–manager!). Writers were no longer the leading force and it was the actor–manager who would garner a reputation for himself and his company.

Theatre under the stewardship of the actor–manager became declamatory in style, often melodramatic and audience pleasing rather than innovative and exciting. However, during this time theatre also began to move back to being a more democratic type of entertainment, with all classes going to see their favourite companies perform their favourite plays. The actor–manager kept his control over theatre for nearly a century, until a new form of theatre began to seep in.

The Russian influence

Perhaps the next major development in theatre came from Russia in the late nineteenth century with the work of the writer Chekhov and the director and actor Stanislavski, who began to pioneer what was then considered a much more realistic type of theatre.

The work of Chekhov and Stanislavski, alongside his collaborator Vladimir Nemirovich Danchenko, both independently and together, began to see a move away from this declamatory style of theatre, leaving the way clear for the many innovations that would come during the rest of the nineteenth and the twentieth centuries. They worked in a more naturalistic style, telling often quite domestic stories. Chekhov is also famous for his 'gun' quote, where he suggests that if you have a loaded rifle on stage in act one, it must be fired by the end of the play. This quote suggests that the craft of writing, or the poetics, was beginning to be explored during the nineteenth century, as ways of creating a more 'natural' form of theatre were explored in both the writing and the performance.

As the art of theatre making was gradually taken more seriously, theatre began to move back into the realm of 'high' culture, with music hall becoming the province of the working class and therefore 'low' culture – meaning that theatre once again became less democratic, less egalitarian, less a mass entertainment. However, the paradox was that at the same time playwrights began to explore the lives of 'ordinary' people more than the lives of kings and gods.

Recent history

The twentieth century saw many changes in theatre movements and styles, and much experimentation, some of which I will explore in more detail in the next chapter on innovation, looking in particular at the work of Bertolt Brecht, Samuel Beckett, Harold Pinter, Joan Littlewood and Caryl Churchill. There was also a variety of theatrical movements, such as the rise of the Angry Young Men, and the Royal Court Theatre assumed an important role as a theatre for new writing. 'Kitchen Sink' dramas and the move away from the more or less exclusive portrayal of the middle and upper classes on stage cultivated a more realistic portrayal of the working class. This was a major pivotal moment for theatre.[4]

Exploring these different movements in theatre history can often be a personal experience, as whilst each is linked to a cultural zeitgeist of the

---

[4] Other movements you might want to explore in more depth include theatre of the absurd, theatre of cruelty, realism, naturalism and surrealism, as well as postmodernism.

time, they can speak to artists now in a variety of ways. One writer might be left completely cold by Ibsen's naturalism, seeing it as a museum piece, whilst another can find it the most important innovation in the whole of theatre history. As an emerging playwright, you will need to find your own way through the history, but it is useful to know about the pivotal moments as a basis for further research.

In terms of theatre's place in society, and how that political with a small 'p' side of theatre came to be so important for theatre makers, there are some practicalities to explore from the last century that impact greatly on how theatre currently works, which should also be considered here.

One of the major innovations in the twentieth century was government subsidy with the creation of the arts council.[5] This led to the building of the National Theatre, the rise and fall and rise and fall (and rise yet again?) of regional theatre and the repertory system, community and youth theatre, fringe theatre and the rise of the artist as entrepreneur. The twentieth century saw some major movements and change in British theatre, and when thinking about defining historic moments, it is clear that some of these can be quite recent and do not necessarily go all the way back to the Ancient Greeks.

> **Joe Sumsion:** The formation of Welfare State Theatre Company, although I think they were just called Welfare State, who were an itinerant company of artists and playmakers. They were interested in the same things Joan Littlewood was interested in but were also interested in spectacle, and air work, so I think Welfare State said theatre can happen anywhere and be anything. They were founded in 1968 and as a practical guidebook their book *Engineers of the Imagination* (1983) has great ideas about making plays.

> Also I suppose the end of the censorship laws (1968), *Look Back In Anger* (1956) at the Royal Court and the start of Kitchen Sink drama, but it has got to be about for me those moments when theatre opened up a whole new audience and a whole new set of things it could say. So here you go, here is a defining moment, and I can say I was there: when *East is East* opened at Stratford East in 1996, and I genuinely believe that that play, and one or two others like it, changed theatre in terms of who it was for and what it represented, who it represented to those audiences. And when it manages to reflect the experience of the new audience it has opened up to.

---

[5] Today, the arts council is split into regions, so there is Arts Council England (ACE), Arts Council for Northern Ireland, Arts Council Wales and Creative Scotland.

We also have this rule of thumb, often if a community is denied or doesn't have access to express itself through arts, or a point of view has been submerged or withheld, when it finds its expression often it has a particular power. It may not be polished, but if its ideas have been held down, when you let them out, they have a vivacity, and that was true of *East is East*.

The ability for theatre makers to create independently without being linked to aristocratic patronage or commercial concerns was a key moment in theatre history because it gave creative freedom, leading to further innovation and change. Many of the great playwrights mentioned above and explored in either Chapter 2 or Chapter 8 worked within this freedom for the first time, and this is important for the emerging playwright to understand. The post–World War II era in the UK, as well as Europe and the USA was an incredibly fertile time creatively, partly because of the lessons learnt from wartime, but also because of the idea of state-subsidised art.

As already mentioned, this is a real whistle-stop tour of the history of theatre, and I will have inevitably left some important aspects out, so here are some other moments in time worth considering:

> **Suzanne Bell:** There's also [...] the Expressionist period in mainland Europe, not so much in the UK, the Absurdist period, the Existentialist period, then of course you can't get away from 1956 and *Look Back In Anger*, but what I find fascinating is that there's a lot of writing about giving eras a name but that only represents a minority of the work that was produced in that time. So you can say, yes the 1990s theatre with like Anthony Neilson and Mark Ravenhill and Sarah Kane, well that was 'In yer face' theatre which is the term that's bandied about but there were loads of other writers happening then and working then, and writing and putting work on. The risk is that it becomes reductive because you're not looking at the breadth of work that is out there and what audiences respond to.

This risk should be borne in mind throughout this book: always remember that in theatre there may be movements that seem to encapsulate an era but there will also be a breadth of other equally valid work being produced that may not fit into a particular movement but which was an important part of the cultural diet of society nonetheless.

As I said at the start of this chapter, the old truism that history is written by the victors is there for a reason, and the purpose of this chapter is to give you a framework in which to further your research into the type of theatre you are interested in, the type of theatre you want to make and therefore the type of theatre that has gone before that you can relate to.

Steven Luckie: The sixteenth century, Shakespeare, and the phrase All the World's a Stage – and that is it. If he worked out that all the world's a stage, then you have to have a good understanding of the world and its make up, so he really did illuminate the absolute power of theatre. And he nicked everything. Tragedy: because he was connected to the court, you don't have to be connected to the court nowadays, you just watch the fall of Margaret Thatcher, at some point the fall of David Cameron, Tony Blair. But he was in the court and so he understood the importance of tragedy, and what that can do, theatre could be epic. They didn't have movies in those days, but they didn't need them because he was doing all this just by writing. Universal, it can appeal to anybody, so it doesn't matter if you live in Guatemala, if you can translate Shakespeare into your language you can begin to understand that this guy really understood universal convention. More importantly he used the same tools as we have today to tell his stories. Shakespeare's voice is a bit like British culture, it has everything, which is why it is so rich. Everything.

In the twentieth century, Brecht. Because it is modern, epic, universal, down came the fourth wall,[6] and most importantly: political. I am talking about the writers and what they were doing, you can relate the writers to what was happening around them, which had such a profound effect, it was the catalyst to their extraordinary writing.

The same century, Pinter in the 1960s, stylisation, a reaction to the Lord Chamberlain, and the liberation that came with the end of censorship – it is just great writing, and I am sure he will come back into fashion. It was great writing, watch all of his stuff. And really, really stylised. What basically Pinter was saying was: you can write differently.

Twenty-first century, final one: Debbie Tucker Green. You can pick out the box: I may be black, but I don't have to write like a black person, I can just write. And the reason she can is that she understands the rules. If you want to change the world, which is what we all set out to do, you have to understand the world we want to change. If you don't do this, you may as well forget it.

When I come across new emerging writers, and they are not always young, the first thing I tell them is that if you want to change the world, you need to understand the world that you want to change. You need to know what the rules are.

---

[6] The fourth wall can be considered to be the imaginary wall between the stage and the audience in a more traditional three-sided 'box' set on a stage.

Take someone like Thatcher – she understood the rules. She understood how Parliament works, she understood how men work, and it is frightening what came about; the way she was treated as a young female MP was appalling, but then look at what came about – she became a man. She took extraordinary advantage of it, and we are still living with that legacy today, and I fundamentally disagree with her policies, but in order to execute them she had to understand the rules, and she did so much better than most of our current politicians.

So I have chosen four playwrights and I have chosen what I think were the events of their time, because Shakespeare used all of these historical events, to articulate the world. And I go back to the person I think had the greater understanding, and I don't know how he did it, because he nicked everything.

I encourage all writers to nick as much as they can, steal! As Dennis Potter used to say, a playwright will eat their own young if they're any good.

There are only so many stories you can tell.

Discovering a history you can relate to can be a very personal journey, as these next four theatre makers explain, but in thinking about the idea of all those post-World War II innovations I mentioned above, see how many references there are to the work of the 1950s and 1960s:

Billy Cowan: For me the avant-garde theatre of the 1920s – Stanislaw Witkiewicz, Brecht, Artaud, Pirandello – was a defining period when experimentation with form really extended the notion of what theatre/a play was. The fifties and sixties were an amazing time for theatre as well and many of my favourites come from this period – Beckett, Pinter, Orton, Peter Barnes, Albee, Osbourne – again there was experimentation with form as well as content and style – with a healthy disregard for naturalism.

Elizabeth Newman: I still think that some of the fundamental moments in British theatre were *Look Back In Anger* (1956) and *Entertaining Mr Sloane* (1964), Edward Bond's *Saved* (1965), the arrival of Sarah Kane, the arrival of Howard Barker, the arrival of Caryl Churchill. All of these have formed the theatre landscape and people have responded and followed the trends. I think Martin Crimp has played an important part in the theatre landscape, because he's not overly vocal about his own importance, I believe (and not just because I have directed it!) that *Attempts On Her Life* (1997) sculpted a new form of theatre: he made it possible to do this and it still be a satisfying audience experience.

There are the key theatre moments, Shakespeare, the Restoration, that have shifted the looking glass of how we look at society, but I relate that to the writer, because I work in a writer's theatre. I wouldn't be a director if there weren't words written down on the page, even devising I need a written down stimulus, I can't work without words. For me, the writer is god, not that the writer is without flaws or need of assistance, but I don't have a job as a director without a writer – the story comes from the writer.

Lizzie Nunnery: I do come back to the idea of Joan Littlewood walking from London to Manchester. Maybe she never got there, maybe it's half myth, but her commitment to creating something new and for the people, and her re-invention of what could be popular, was so significant. I think John McGrath's *A Good Night Out* is an incredibly significant moment, and the two link together in my mind. His recognition of working class forms as valuable in theatre is essential. I can't quite imagine theatre without that having happened. Shelagh Delaney's *A Taste of Honey* was also really important. All these things are associated for me. People talk about *Look Back In Anger* as this incredibly liberating moment for theatre, but I feel that as a text now that feels less relevant – the anger isn't connected enough for it to stay really resonant. Whereas Delaney's style of writing that held a mirror up to real people and didn't make them voice boxes in any way – I think that did so much more to allow working class stories to flourish on stage, and to allow a new freedom in approaching character: writing characters who might seem ugly or in some ways appalling without criticising them or creating voyeurism. In my opinion part of the bad legacy of some of the working class plays since the sixties is a kind of voyeurism of working class people and of poverty, and Shelagh Delaney is an amazing example of someone who just knew it and wrote it and said something very profound about what it meant to be those people at those times.

Kevin Dyer: We are told that there are big defining moments aren't we? I think Shakespeare probably was, I think the 1950s in Britain probably was, I think probably Absurdist theatre, Beckett in the late 1950s/1960s. I think the growing number of black writers that has happened in Britain and in the USA since the 1970s is a defining moment, but I do think we are currently in a golden age of theatre, because there are more and more people writing, which means there are more and more voices, and more people writing about more and more stuff.

Now we know that there is no career structure for a playwright. You don't have to be rich to write anymore, you can be great at the age of 17 or a great writer at the age of 57. Sometimes it is the structures around writing that have been very important, like the National Theatre has been really important, the Royal Court was really important, all the universities across that UK that teach creative writing and give space where people can write – that's very, very important. You know, I was born in 1957, and when I was a lad on a council estate, the idea of being a writer was an impossibility, it really was an impossibility. It is now more of a possibility for more people, and that social change has been a great turning point.

Companies like the Theatre Centre, companies like the Women's Theatre Group and Black Theatre Co-op, which doesn't exist anymore, all those political companies of the 1970s and 1980s, you know they did not always make the best work but they were a place where people with politics could write and could learn to be theatre makers.

The historic moments in theatre depend on who you are; we all find our own defining moments depending on what our interests are, our gender, our class, our culture. For me, one of the big defining moments was when I went to Iran and I saw theatre in Iran, I don't know if it was defining for anyone else, but it was for me.

Writers and theatre makers find historical pivotal moments for themselves, moments that they can relate to, which then feeds into how they themselves work. For this reason, the playwright needs to understand theories, understand what particular theatre makers are attempting to do at particular moments in time to be able to critically analyse what those defining moments in history mean for your own creativity as well as understanding the wider cultural landscape you will be working in.

The above insights are also central to the reason I have chosen to speak to theatre makers who are working to create new theatre work now. In terms of critical explorations of making theatre, there are as many arguments as there are writers, or theatre makers, and all of them will have a slightly different point of view. And this is fine and right and as it should be – this is what makes theatre such an exciting and dynamic place to work. Theatre thrives on difference, on different ideas and different ways of working, and yet you will always find someone who will collaborate with you to tell a story. Finding those moments in theatre history that you respond to as a writer will take some research and a bit of work, but when you do discover those exciting innovators of the past, some of whom we will be exploring in the next chapter, you will find that this shapes your own work, strengthening your understanding of what 'playwrighting' means, as well as enabling you to contextualise the important role theatre has played in almost every culture across the world and throughout time, and therefore the tradition you are joining when starting out as a new playwright.

2 The Cultures of Writing for Theatre – Innovators

In this chapter I am going to build on the history of theatre explored in Chapter 1 by looking at some specific playwrights who changed the way theatre worked, contextualising their innovations within their own time and thinking critically about how and why their innovations still matter. The choice of innovative writers is based upon those the interviewees mentioned as important to them. Of course, some have mentioned directors and dramaturgs, who you may also want to explore as further research, but as this is a book about writing for theatre, I have concentrated on theatre writers for this part.

Some of these names may be new to you whilst others you may already be aware of, but it is always a good idea to read their plays, read interviews and books about them, but more importantly try to see their work in a theatre space or, if that is impossible, on a screen. Contextualise these playwrights, try to imagine what theatre was like before their work came to prominence and then take on board how theatre has changed since their innovations. At the end of this chapter there is also a short section on those that emerging playwrights can learn from. These may not be traditional innovators but they may offer more practical suggestions in terms of craft and development.

Asking theatre makers who they consider to be the most important theatre innovators was incredibly enlightening. Many of them did speak of the 'usual suspects', ones you may already know, such as Shakespeare, Ibsen and Pinter, all of whom are incredibly important, but we all have our own favourites, with different reasons for choosing them. Sometimes the term 'innovator' itself can be a difficult one. Lizzie Nunnery, for example, felt she could not give a definitive answer, Suzanne Bell said she could think of so many, and Ruth Little said she did not have a 'single number one ranking for that title'.

If innovator is quite a difficult term, why have I chosen to use it? Well, it is a term that is accepted, certainly academically, when talking about cultures of theatre and its history, but for this chapter my meaning leans towards

those playwrights who, within their society in their own time, moved theatre in a different direction, who somehow changed what was happening in
their time, no matter how small that change was. Many of the interviewees
spoke about people who are also making new and exciting theatre now as
well as in the past. Innovators have therefore been split into two groups: the
first, in this chapter, are what I will term innovators of the past, whilst the
second, explored in Chapter 8, are the innovators of the present (and possibly the future).

Innovators of the past

How far back into the past should I go? Well, theatre still respects and works
with Aristotle's Unities, so I think it is fair to say we should go no farther
back than that.

> **Suzanne Bell:** It still blows my mind that 2,500 years ago Aristotle wrote
> *Poetics* and we still adhere to that because that's the fundamentals of
> storytelling for an audience and the communication to an audience
> through a story. And however that story is told, in whatever form, in what-
> ever innovation, those people still all go back to Aristotle, so you could
> go: well, he's the innovator, because he's lasted 2,500 years. I am a big
> Shakespeare geek as well; I was listening to Radio 4 on the way over here
> and they were talking about the Othello remix at the Globe to Globe
> festival which came through the Shakespeare Theatre in Chicago and I
> remember when I was training as a young director and I was at the Oxford
> School of Drama, they had a group of American students come over and
> they used to rap Shakespeare because they got the rhythm, and that really
> unhooked something in Shakespeare for me. But yeah, Aristotle.

> **Steven Luckie:** Shakespeare. It is open to critical debate, but because
> he really understood the world in which he was working, and you can
> see this in the devices he was using. It doesn't matter you who are, it
> really doesn't matter if you're Pakistani, if you're black, whatever, read
> all 34 plays and you will find something in there, and if you don't then
> there's something profoundly wrong with you! If you can't be inspired by
> Shakespeare, then there's something wrong with you!

Aristotle and Shakespeare laid down many of the 'rules' of theatre we live
with, or write against, today, but they can be quite difficult for people new to
theatre to access as innovators. They are part of what is known as 'the canon',
a collection of Western literature that academics deemed so important that

it has helped to form Western culture as we know it – so how can they also be innovative? Of course Aristotle and Shakespeare are talking to us from a long way back in history, and their innovations no longer seem innovative precisely because they belong to the classical canon. Very often the reason students are 'turned off' theatre is because in school the only plays they read were Shakespeare, droning through a dreary lesson wondering how on earth this 500 year old writer could be in any way relevant to them now. As quite a few interviewees suggest in Chapter 3, seeing a Shakespeare play with the school can often be someone's first experience of theatre, either good or bad, yet here I am quoting current theatre makers as saying Shakespeare is an innovator. But the fact of the matter is: he was. He may seem inaccessible now, but the work he did in terms of theatrical devices, characterisation and the use of language cannot be ignored if being a playwright is an ambition of yours. The Renaissance, as suggested in Chapter 1, was an incredibly fertile time creatively, but the prolific work of Shakespeare spoke, as Luckie says, to his audience and their experience. He wrote of his time and his world, creating believable characters and asking questions of his contemporary audience, many of which are still relevant today. There are many books on Shakespeare, and there is little point in me rehashing their main themes, but reading Shakespeare as a writer, as a playwright, you can learn about his use of plot and structure, as well as the very well-known fact that he collected stories from elsewhere and re-imagined them in his plays. He understood that there are perhaps 'no new stories' as the truism goes, but what he did was to re-create those stories in his own voice. By putting two or more of those stories together, using them to create subplots giving a rich background to the main plot, by fleshing out the characters, giving them nuance and complicated inner lives, he worked as any modern writer should. He was also collaborative, forming part of the theatre company and working with or writing for particular actors. Seeing these plays performed can give the new playwright a wholly different sense of what 'theatrical' is and can be, in terms of structure, storytelling and audience experience. Many theatres will put on productions of Shakespeare plays in their season, often to get in that school audience, so it is worth going to see these, but do try to find one that speaks to you in some way. This could be because it has an all-female cast, or a celebrity actor you particularly like, or it is a youth theatre version that has somehow been reworked. Allow your ear to tune into the language slowly, perhaps read the play beforehand, and consider all the elements of theatrical device that are being utilised in this production, such as the set, the costumes or the actors' way of speaking. It might even help to write up your experience in your notebook as quickly as you can afterwards, because attempting to love Shakespeare is a good first step for any new playwright. A really good book to read to try and get to grips with the importance of Shakespeare is *Backwards and Forwards* by David Ball (1983) which explores the play *Hamlet* in some detail but relates this exploration to making and creating theatre now.

> **Billy Cowan:** I find the word innovator to be problematic because it's so difficult really to pin down 'new methods, ideas' etc. to one person. For example, Ibsen is often credited as the father of mimetic theatre – naturalistic, psychological realism – yet Strindberg also wrote realistic plays to begin with and Shakespeare's characters are also psychologically real. It's impossible to have a hierarchy with someone named as the most important. There's been many important practitioners/theorists – Artaud, Witkiewicz, Strindberg, Ibsen, Brecht, Beckett, Meyerhold for example, who've all developed theatre. There's also important people who've been forgotten like the playwright Peter Barnes.

> **Hannah Tyrrell-Pinder:** It's probably someone who I would no longer think of as an innovator because they've changed theatre so much that it's just the way theatre is now – someone like Harold Pinter or Joan Littlewood, or whoever originally set up the Everyman and Playhouse and created that vibe and that energy, with all the young talent that was coming through. It wouldn't be someone like Stanislavski that is more method or theatre based, it would more be someone who did something that theatre shifted on its axis a little bit and now that just seems normal.

Tyrrell-Pinder gets to the heart of what I am looking for in an innovator here, someone who has changed theatre so much that now it is just the norm. Cowan mentions quite a few playwrights and it is worth exploring – albeit briefly – the reasons why these people are so important. I have split this section into nineteenth century and twentieth century innovators. The three playwrights I will explore from the nineteenth century are not British playwrights, but are arguably the most innovative (see Cowan's comments above for that argument!) and influential on British theatre of that era, as well as being names I have already mentioned, so you may have started to look into their work already.

Nineteenth-century innovators

Henrik Ibsen was a Norwegian playwright who is perhaps best known for plays such as *A Doll's House, Ghosts* and *Hedda Gabler*. He asked many questions about the world he was living in, and often wrote female characters who questioned the societal norms they were part of.

Lizzie Nunnery: The most influential for me is probably Ibsen. I think his brand of naturalism that also completely embraces poeticism is so exciting; his way of writing about ordinary people; his way of taking on the micro and making it so significant – creating a macro for his plays that lives with you and remains relevant over generations. I think the imprint of what he did remains in so much contemporary work. And actually he was a lot stranger that people give him credit for. His later plays got much less naturalistic and did a lot more unusual things with character, voice and set. Actually he's not just about drawing rooms and sofas. But what he did with those contained situations, those small households, small families – the way he managed to create a sense of the whole world and what makes us human through those situations – I keep going back to.

Thinking about the time Ibsen was writing in is crucial to contextualising why he is so important, as it is about any historic writer or theatre maker: the innovation comes with the time and place they were creating the work in.

Rob Drummer: I am a real theatre geek, and I remember finding out about, if not the first, certainly one of the first performances of *A Doll's House* in London. Often new plays would receive their London premiere as a matinee performance, and it was an audience characterised by being predominately female, because that was the only opportunity to go to theatre at the time without a chaperone, without a husband or a father. So what you get as *A Doll's House* rolls into town is an audience full of women – sisters, mothers, daughters and friends. I remember reading this great contemporary account – which I am going to massively para-phrase – from a man who had been watching, and he bemoans the fact that the matinee is full of hats that the women are wearing, so he can't see the stage properly, and the rustling of chocolates, all these things that the women do who are engaging with the theatre. And what is profound as a moment of theatre history is that you have a play, and whether or not you think Ibsen is or isn't a feminist, he has written a play that is of course controversial and of course provocative, playing in front of a room full of women, who may or may not be having these sorts of conversations, but who are suddenly confronted with this fabulously strong portrayal of a woman on stage. And at the end of that play, you just imagine what that crowd of women are thinking and feeling, and then leaving the theatre and going off and having tea, and talking to more women. What happens is that the run of that play is pulled, but it becomes a tension, there is a piece of work in town that is daring to put a new perspective on stage. So as a moment of theatre history and thinking about new plays, that is a moment that sticks with me.

As a side note, it is interesting to see in these two quotes how a writer (Nunnery) and a dramaturg (Drummer) each approaches Ibsen and his importance. Nunnery explores Ibsen's writing style, whilst Drummer explores the effect the play had on an audience, and this, in a microcosm, is how the work of the writer and the dramaturg/director divides. As a playwright you must be aware of both aspects of theatre making, the words on the page and the audience experience, but there is always the expectation that as a playwright you will lean more towards the words on the page. This is another reason I have chosen to collaborate here with directors and dramaturgs as well as writers, to give you a more rounded sense of what writing for theatre and theatre making can mean.

In broad terms then, theatre during the nineteenth century was still centred on the classics, with a declamatory acting style telling the stories of kings and courtiers. Ibsen, by contrast, wrote plays about ordinary people. They were still middle-class people, but they were not aristocracy. Often their worlds and their problems were quite small, but the point Nunnery makes about writing the micro whilst exploring the macro is crucial to understanding Ibsen's importance: the ability to ask wider social questions through what appears to be a domestic drama using heightened naturalistic dialogue is the innovation Ibsen brought to theatre.

This is an important ability for writers or theatre makers; the stage space you have can be quite small, and if you stick to Aristotle's Unities you may be aiming for just one or two locations, and yet you are being asked to pose questions about your society, your community, the wider world, within this small space. This is why the technique of exploring the macro (the wider world) through the micro (the small and often domestic story) can still work for playwrights. In *A Doll's House* Nora's world is confined to being a good wife and mother and being socially supportive to her husband who sees himself as a potential pillar of the community. Unwittingly, she has broken the law to support the husband she loves when he was ill; when she confesses this crime to him to avoid being blackmailed, his first thought is of his social standing, not of his wife and family. The criticisms of the social rules and the actual laws making women of Nora's time second-class citizens are clear in this domestic tale, showing how the macro in the micro works. That this had not been put on a stage before highlights the reason Ibsen is so revered by playwrights and theatre makers, whether you 'like' his plays or not. And learning to understand and contextualise this type of innovative theatre making forms part of your critical engagement with theatre. Go beyond what you 'like' and analyse what a particular play does within its historical, social and political context.

As Cowan mentions above, **August Strindberg** was a Swedish playwright born some 20 years after Ibsen, but his work was being produced around the same time as Ibsen's, his most famous play being *Miss Julie*. He also wrote in a naturalistic style and was influenced by the work of French writer Emile Zola. He is perhaps no longer considered to be as much an innovator as Ibsen, but his work is certainly worth exploring for similar micro/macro reasons and the way contemporary society is portrayed.

Anton Chekhov, a Russian writer, worked with Konstantin Stanislavski, a Russian actor and director, and is traditionally thought of as a major innovator, with both often taught as such across creative writing and performing arts programmes, as I touched on in Chapter 1. Again, if you contextualise their work in their society during the nineteenth century, then they undoubtedly were innovators, but there is a sense that their work has been elevated in terms of innovation above many others of their time, others who were also trying to push boundaries and find new ways of creating theatre such as Danchenko, who is rarely mentioned even though he collaborated with them. Famously, Lee Strasberg built on Stanislavksi's ideas to create 'The Method' or method acting, but context again is all for Chekhov and Stanislavski. They changed the way theatre worked in terms of collaboration between writer and director and the way the script could be interpreted by the actors.

As with Shakespeare, their work and ideas can seem old fashioned now, but it is important to remember the historic context and see, for example, the change from that declamatory acting style, to the more realistic method of acting that Stanislavski brought, especially when working on Chekhov's plays.

Also, as mentioned in Chapter 1, Chekhov started to explore the craft of writing through critical analysis, and this brought the craft of the playwright into focus. Discussion around how plays were structured, what plays could be about and audience expectations took place. Of course, reading a Chekhov play now may seem like a Russian history lesson, but have a look at other work being produced at this time, analyse what the writer is doing in terms of character, structure and plot, and use this analysis for either further creative work or critical analysis of some perhaps lesser known plays or writers from history.

Twentieth-century innovators

The twentieth century saw many innovations in theatre style and theory, perhaps more so than the nineteenth century. The following innovators have already been mentioned by the interviewees, and most of these are generally accepted to be innovators, but again there may be many others that you find in your own research who speak to you more directly.

Antonin Artaud was a French playwright and director who worked during the first half of the twentieth century and who proposed the theory of 'Theatre of Cruelty', which simply put, was a form of theatre that shattered the suspension of disbelief, or that which is not real. Artaud had a nihilistic view of the world and explored his understanding of theatre in his book *Theatre And Its Double,* originally published in 1938.

Bertolt Brecht was a German writer and director active from 1920 until his death in 1956, although from the mid 1940s his work rate declined along with his health. A committed Marxist, Brecht conceived of a type of theatre which tried to remove the idea of catharsis or emotional engagement from the audience, instead wanting them to engage intellectually with the ideas explored in the plays. His way of doing this was to use a variety of techniques aimed at reminding the audience that what they were watching was not reality but merely a representation of such, through the use of slogans, banners, costume choice and projection, amongst other devices. His theory, *Verfremdungseffekt,* has no direct translation into English, but is known variously as estrangement effect, alienation effect or distancing effect – none of which quite capture the original meaning – but was an attempt to make the audience think about the themes and messages in the play rather than being carried along by the story on an emotional level.

Brecht worked across Europe and many of his plays still have revivals, including *Caucasian Chalk Circle* (1944), *Mother Courage* (1939) and *The Threepenny Opera* (1928) which he wrote in collaboration with composer Kurt Weill. This play was based on Gay's *The Beggar's Opera* – again showing the importance for a writer to know their theatre history – and contains the very famous 'Mack The Knife' song. The innovation of reminding the audience that none of what they are watching is real, that they need to engage intellectually rather than emotionally, is perhaps not something many writers would attempt now, but Brecht was rejecting Aristotle's Unities and the naturalism of Stanislavski in what is termed 'epic' theatre. In this the audience are always made aware that they are watching a play through a series of devices such as projection, commentary, even the use of a chorus, and it is useful to understand how this concept was an innovation, as the terms 'Brechtian' and 'epic' theatre are still often used to describe modern productions, often interchangeably.[1]

---

[1] Although this is not quite correct, because Epic theatre was also pioneered during the early- to mid-twentieth century by other theatre makers such as Piscator and Meyerhold.

So, whilst these techniques and innovations continue to be tied to their historic time and place, as well as their social and political context, their influence in simply allowing writers to experiment with these ideas can continue to be seen today.

Samuel Beckett was an Irish writer who was active from the mid 1930s until the 1960s, and is often considered one of the first post-modernists. As a young man, he had the opportunity to work with James Joyce, which had a profound effect on him, and in turn Beckett had a profound effect on Harold Pinter, one of the great innovative playwrights of the twentieth century. Beckett spent most of his life in France, writing in both English and French, and won the Nobel Prize for Literature in 1969. He is probably most famous for his play *Waiting for Godot* (1953) which is often held up as an example of a play that is about 'nothing'. He worked in what is now known as Theatre of the Absurd, which advocates a nihilistic view of life, meaning that dialogue often has no meaning or is not logical. He also wrote poetry and prose, but other theatre works of Beckett include *Endgame* (1957), *Krapp's Last Tape* (1958) and *Happy Days* (1961).

Joan Littlewood is a name that came up several times with those I interviewed.

> **Joe Sumsion:** The figure who would come to mind would be Joan Littlewood. As an innovator, she started the Theatre Royal, Stratford East, and at the time when she was directing theatre was, as I understand it, generally speaking middle and upper middle class sport. She thought about community, and that link connecting people on the stage and the people in the audience. And she felt that link, or that loop, because it is not just a one direction flow, it is not just about the people on stage giving to the people in the audience, it is what is on the stage being reflective of the people in the audience, and that was shown in productions such as *Oh, What A Lovely War!* I worked at the Theatre Royal in Stratford East in 1994 for a year, 40 years on, and then the borough of Newham had just become the first majority ethnic minority borough in England, and we were still asking ourselves the question: how can what is on this stage be reflective of the community we serve? And that meant we had to put on work that reflected those communities, so when I was there *East is East* premiered at Stratford East to a majority, I would say 80%, Asian audience, and you knew that the majority of these people had never been to the theatre before. And so her influence remained at that theatre, but actually it remains here at this theatre (The Dukes, Lancaster) as well, as I still believe in that.

Littlewood was an English director who worked during the middle part of the twentieth century, until the 1970s. She worked with both text and devised work, and is probably best known for her championing of the young playwright **Shelagh Delaney** (*A Taste of Honey*, 1958) and political musicals such as *Fings Ain't What They Used To Be* (1959) and *Oh, What A Lovely War!* (1965). Littlewood pioneered the idea of the theatre workshop in which the text was not a solid thing that was unchangeable, but could be explored to create the best possible piece of theatre. This is often a useful tool for writers to use now, whether in terms of devising or developing a piece of work. She was also, as Sumsion mentions above, rooted in the idea of theatre for the community, which links to much issue based or political theatre made right up to the present day.

Zosia Wand's innovator, for example, is also a director who has continued to champion devising work:

> **Zosia Wand:** Max Stafford Clark because of his workshopping process; I am really interested in collaborative working, and I think theatre is a brilliant place to explore that, because it is a sort of collaboration between the audience and the people on stage, but I just really like the idea that designers, actors and composers can all be involved in creating a piece as well. All that input is really stimulating. I don't find it quite as stimulating to produce a script and then hand it over and not be involved in the next stage of the process. And that's not wanting to be in control of the whole process, I love handing something over, but I just want to be there to see what goes on after that. I like cross-art form work as well, I think it is really stimulating to talk to people who are creative and artistic in different media, and the sparks that happen illuminate your work, and make you think about a different way to tell a story. So with Max Stafford Clark I like the way he is prepared to experiment and give writers time to explore things and connect with other artists. It is a big risk, and he's prepared to take that risk. I was reading his book recently, the Case Studies that he's written, and the number of times they opened a play and he had no idea if it was going to work, even at that stage, and I think that takes such guts, such courage, and that is what makes theatre really exciting.

Max Stafford Clark founded Joint Stock and Out of Joint theatre companies as well as having spent time as the Artistic Director of the Royal Court, and is still working today.

Harold Pinter continued to explore absurdist theatre, hugely influenced by Samuel Beckett, becoming more political in his work during his later years. His body of work is enormous, but as a starting point you could explore *The Birthday Party* (1957), *The Caretaker* (1959), *The Homecoming* (1964), *Betrayal* (1978) and *One For The Road* (1984). Pinter's use of language and silence, as well as his structuring and use of repetition, all work towards an often uncomfortable experience for the audience, highlighting the wider questions the playwright is asking in his piece. If you consider a play to be the very tip of an iceberg, with all the subtext and backstory existing below the surface, Pinter was a master of his craft. What often seems meaningless conversation hints at a sense of menace, of awkwardness, of tension between the characters. Nothing is ever what it seems and no one ever says what they mean.

In 2005, Pinter was awarded the Nobel Prize for Literature and he was active from the mid 1950s until his death in 2008, his last piece of work being the screenplay for the remake of *Sleuth* (2007).

Caryl Churchill should perhaps not be in the 'innovators of the past' section at all because she is, of course, still working. However she became linked with the Royal Court in the 1970s and her (arguably) most famous work *Top Girls* was written in 1982, so she just about fits in the twentieth century innovators section.

Churchill's career is fascinating to trace through her writing, because by analysing her works in a linear fashion you can see how her writing became less realistic, more fantastical and more theatrical. From experiments with overlapping dialogue in *Top Girls,* to a play that has no order or story, the structure of which is left up to the production team, such as *Love and Information* (2012), the reason Churchill is considered an innovator is most probably due to her constant theatrical experimentation as well as her interest in political and feminist issues explored through her work.

Joe Orton was born in 1933 and was murdered by his partner in 1967, but during his short life he made a great impact on theatre and theatre writing. His writing was based in the genre of farce, and yet he used this genre to write of the darker side of human nature and wrote satirically about the society he was part of. Openly gay at a time when to be so was illegal, Orton was a personality of the swinging sixties scene, living his life as something of an artwork. His writing is funny, vicious and highlighted uncomfortable truths about his society which still ring true today.

The need for the playwright to engage critically with cultural debates about, for example, absurdist theatre versus naturalistic theatre, the micro or the epic representing the macro and the suspension of disbelief versus *Verfremdungseffeckt* is crucial to grounding oneself in the theatre-making tradition. Also crucial is knowing and understanding what tools there are in your toolbox for creating new work rather than trying to re-invent a wheel that rolled by long ago. Looking at the work of these innovators, amongst others, can help the emerging playwright to see the possibilities of using theatre as a creative medium, to understanding how form can affect story, how constant experimentation is the key to good writerly practice and how the stories of failure and success can keep us going when it seems impossible to write yet another draft! But also it is important to note that these playwrights are innovators because they cared about the society they lived in, they wanted to ask questions of it, create art not just for the sake of art but to examine the world around them and then to ask their audiences to do the same.

Who else can new playwrights learn from?

During our conversations about writing new theatre, I also asked interviewees who they thought new playwrights could actively learn from, in terms of form and theatricality, people who may not be seen as innovators perhaps but who are working writers with a long career and variety of work. Some of these may or may not be famous playwrights, but they were the names that were genuinely put forward by those who currently make exciting theatre. Again some people looked back in time whilst others looked forward and to the present.

> **Hannah Tyrrell-Pinder:** Arthur Miller. I think *All My Sons* is a really, really good play, well crafted, and well structured, it still stands up to scrutiny. But anything by Arthur Miller, because he just writes really well-crafted plays that are moving and still relevant now. I'd also add Brian Friel to the list, I'm a big fan of Brian Friel, he uses language really well and in the majority of his plays he does politics with a big P but with a light touch for the most part, with interesting and complex characters, and the language is just so beautiful. *Translations* is one of my favourite ever plays.

> **Elizabeth Newman:** Writers need to go back further than contemporary playwrights, to the Ibsens and Chekhovs. I would ban new playwrights from reading Simon Stephens because if I read one more rip-off play I might shoot myself – we went through the same thing with Harold Pinter, didn't we? Because it is a particular rhythm that seems to permeate the brain, but if they are a brilliant writer of dialogue then all they need to do is expand their understanding of how to give the audience a satisfying experience, so I would also get them to read the American plays, because these are less copyable, and with Ibsen and Chekhov, they're adaptations so they can't copy it! Reading all the different versions of *The Seagull,* for example, would give a whole idea of structure and story form, they could read Martin Crimp's Seagull, David Hare's – read a whole array.

American writers such as Tennessee Williams, Sam Shepard, David Mamet and Tony Kushner are all worth reading and could as easily be the innovator names in the list above if I were looking to the USA rather than to Europe. Newman's point was about giving the audience a good experience and this is something that all these writers do well, and learning how to do that too through analysing what these playwrights are doing on the page is a vital part of being a playwright. And this again highlights the idea I keep returning to: the historical story of theatre is instilled in all theatre makers and this is something new playwrights simply cannot escape. In the early days, as Newman also points out, it is easy to be overly influenced by one particular playwright that you respond well to. The answer to this is to read and analyse a breadth of work, learn from old masters, learn from contemporary writers, learn from as yet unpublished and unproduced plays, learn from your peers and learn from the world around you.

> **Chris Thorpe:** [New playwrights] can learn from reading the writers they really like, they can learn from their contemporaries, they can learn from reading the classics – there are so many plays out there, that if you want to write plays that have this incredible classical structure, then learn that. It depends on what kind of playwright you want to be – because there are as many answers to that question as there are playwrights. But I think what you can learn to do is talk to people, it doesn't matter if they're theatre people, just talk to people, find out what obsesses them and what obsesses you and try to find the common ground between those two things and a way of expressing that.

3   Establishing Practice

This chapter will explore what writing for theatre means in practice and why playwrights want to write for theatre – and yes, I am going to explore this area before I even begin to look at character, story, plot and dialogue. Why? Simply because any writer should be aware of the medium they are aiming to work in, and theatre can be a tricky one to get to grips with if you are not already a theatre geek, although I hope you are on your way to being one by now.

Theatre has to inspire curiosity, a passion to explore your world and a need to produce new ideas, new ways of telling your story. You can often hear those who work in theatre lament how very badly it pays, and it may seem that writing for theatre can be a thankless task. So why would anyone do it? In this chapter theatre makers explain their reasons for wanting to be creatively involved in making productions happen and examine why theatre is important to them.

What is theatre for?

For me as a writer, theatre is the most exciting collaborative art form to be involved with, and one of the more creatively fascinating aspects is being able to sit in the auditorium and be part of the audience reception of your play, which is as terrifying as it is exciting. It is important to me because of the creative experimentation that can happen in the theatre space, the new ways of telling a story and the importance of being able to bring in issues around social change, exploring what it means to live in your society today, and sharing this with new audiences. I asked people what they thought the importance of theatre is today, what it means to them and what theatre is for. I asked these questions because a writer needs an understanding of this. If you write a novel, you know it is for escapism, on the train commute or by the holiday poolside. If you write for a soap you know you are writing for relaxation and escapism after a hard day's work. But theatre makes its audience work with it. So what is it for? What does it mean?

Joe Sumsion: [Theatre] means community, ideas, self-expression and I don't just mean mine; it means expressing the human condition, if that's not overcooking it.

In terms of my role here in the theatre, if you take Lancaster University and The Dukes out of Lancaster, it would be a very, very different city. Because one of the things The Dukes does in this community, it stands as a celebration of creativity and it stands as a celebration of the arts, but it also stands as a kind of independence. Lancaster is quite an independent-minded place, so the idea that within Lancaster there is a home for people to make up and tell stories, and for Lancaster people (of which I am one) to decide which stories we make up and tell for our community. And we have a fantastic Young People's theatre here, where those young people are in charge of their own stories and telling them in interesting ways, I sort of believe that you could argue that the ability to make up and tell your own stories is an essential part of a healthy community. The Dukes is interesting because we've got lots of different ways to tell stories, so we're a cinema as well as a theatre, we put on young people's work and other art forms such as dance and music.

There is evidence of people moving to Lancaster because of coming to shows in Williamson Park, people come to that, like it and decide to live here – so what does that tell you – they liked Williamson Park, but it also tells you that they like what the place stands for. If you can make good theatre in a wonderful outdoors setting, that is a nearly unique way of making theatre. I have been told myself at least 10 times that story.

This is an incredible feat for a theatre: people move to the city to be near a particular producing venue. But Sumsion's point about a healthy community having the ability to tell their own stories goes back to the basic idea of communal storytelling being a primal trait, innate in all humans. In a nutshell, this is what theatre is for.

In my experience, those who work in theatre recognise that they are lucky to do for a job what many people would do as a hobby or simply for the love of it, but this realisation must not stop any of us from being critical of theatre, both as a cultural entity and individual productions. Seeing the role of theatre as being important to the overall culture of our society, whether that be in smaller communities, large cities or communities of young people, for example, is often the reason many writers choose to become playwrights. Of course, the critical aspects of making theatre can sometimes get lost when speaking of attracting audiences or making money, but these are elements that are in tension with the creative aspects of simply making art.

Artists must engage with what has gone before and be critical of work currently being produced – and this does not necessarily mean being negatively critical – by analysing what works and what does not for a particular audience and whether the effect aimed for has been achieved. Only with this critical engagement can new writers explore how those boundaries can be pushed even more, not just in your own work but in the work of others.

You will note also that the word 'community' often comes up when talking about theatre, and the idea that humans are social beings who need spaces in which to socialise is one of the main arguments for the continuing relevance of theatre, why society needs theatre.

> **Kevin Dyer:** Some people go out on a Friday and get pissed, some people use a lot of drugs to escape reality. For me, I use theatre. Theatre is where we come together as a community, as a society, or as individuals who become a society, through stories. We witness and share stories that help us work the world out. Theatre transports you, as films can and actually as TV can and as reading a book can – what they do is they pull you out of yourself, and at the same time, in another part of your brain, you also look at what's going on inside you, you can't help but do that because you take yourself to the theatre event. So, I love the act of transportation. I try to make theatre which pulls people emotionally out of their little safe place, I don't want to upset them or make them cry, I just want to make them feel things which they wouldn't feel if they were at home, or if they were with their mates, or if they were at work. You know, brighter things, sharper things, more complicated things.

Theatre is a personal shared experience, which sounds oxymoronic, but it is true. The way that actor makes that gesture may affect only you in the audience, but it will be affecting you whilst you are in a room full of people who are also being individually affected by the piece. That emotional context, catharsis, is a vital part of theatre. When real theatre geeks speak about theatre, it can become quite visceral.

> **Holly Race Roughan:** It is like an addiction, I guess; I feel addicted to it. It is not 'my passion'. It connects with my gut, not my head. It means occasion, a communal experience, it means we're still alive. The idea of it not existing freaks me out. When I come across people who have never been to the theatre, my immediate impulse is: oh my god, I've got to take you right now! But in another sense, for theatre to be all those things it has got to be exceptional and there is a lot of good theatre but not much exceptional theatre. Also it is ritualistic, it is about a community coming together to see something put on by other members of their community,

to experience what it means to live in that community they are all in. That can mean just the community of that moment.

Suzanne Bell: Theatre for me is my life and my passion, I begin to atrophy if I don't go and see theatre. But I'm rare; for most people theatre is still something that is a treat and also something that is disposable income, and people's disposable income is being squeezed. There are so many other distractions, so why should 9,000 people come and see your play? I'm not talking about writing something commercially, that's a different thing, what I'm talking about is giving that audience the best experience for their money, and really taking them on a journey, really telling them a surprising story, really making them go: I couldn't see that at the cinema; I couldn't see that on my telly. Has it been worth them giving up their time, which is precious, or giving up their disposable income, which is precious? Is it something they couldn't see or experience in another form or medium? I have Netflix, I can sit and binge on a boxset, why should I get out of my house and come and spend 20 or 25 quid? That's not to say people won't do it, but if you look at why people spend so much money on sporting events or music events it's because of the emotional experience they will have at that event. So a band or a DJ will think about the way they put a set together, to take the audience on a journey, to give them an experience, to give them an emotional experience, to create or evoke in them some emotions and to give them a memorable time, so that they come out of that experience going: that was money well spent. Why did so many people watch Andy Murray in the Wimbledon final in 2013? They weren't tennis fans, they weren't tennis aficionados, it was because that was the best story: will he, won't he? And how can theatre evoke that level of experience in an audience? How can we make them stop breathing, how can we make them cry, how can we make them grasp the hand of the loved one that they're with and tell them they love them, or when they come out of the theatre they have to phone their mum and dad and tell them they love them? Theatre can do that, but an awful lot doesn't. And that is what theatre means for me and is something that I think writers need to really think about. I know Mike Bartlett talks about friends of his who aren't theatre goers who will say to him: is it better than a gig? Cos we'll go and see a gig, but if the experience of your play isn't better than a gig, then why should I come and see your play, because it'll cost a similar amount of money.

Childcare, drinks, dinner, travel, as well as the tickets, you're talking £100 a couple coming to see a show. Who has that kind of money at the end of the month? So it has to be something they want to come and see. And I don't want that to be daunting. I think of it as throwing down the gauntlet for writers, you have got to tell this story, live, now and you're not being passive about. Theatre isn't passive, telly and film are passive experiences for an audience, but theatre is an active experience for an audience. People come wanting to work, wanting to engage, their imagination, their emotions, their intellect, wanting to engage politically. They'll watch a box set if they want to be passive, and it is such a big thing for me when I read scripts and I think: you've forgotten your audience, you're just in your head now. Recognise that theatre is collaborative, and a collaborative challenge to a designer, a director, an audience, an actor to fulfil that vision. The writer is at the heart of that collaboration but it is a collaboration.

Bell goes on to give an example of what she means, and it is interesting how her passion and excitement leaps from the page as she recalls this particular production:

> *Earthquakes* (by Mike Bartlett) in London at the National I loved, it absolutely was playing our journey through it, we felt exhilarated, we stopped breathing. Just before the interval the main character, who is pregnant, and she's freaking out because she thinks the world is going to end and she doesn't want to bring a child into this world, goes to the hospital and says: I need a scan, you have to get rid of this baby, you have to get rid of it. And they say: no it's too late, we can't get rid of it, but we'll scan to check the baby's OK. So they scan it and they have a massive big wall of the scan, and they say, look it's fine, it's all fine. And then the baby's head turned, in this 2-D scan, and the baby's head turned and went 'Noooooo!' Blackout! Interval! The entire audience was silent, and you just go, you did that deliberately. That 10 second gap before the applause of what have we just collectively just shared, this experience? Oh my god, it's amazing – boom! That's the writer, my belief is: that's the writer every time. Because if it's not in the writing, you can't make it from nothing.

Reading these accounts of what theatre can mean to people, reading about the emotions it can evoke, is the best argument for what theatre is for – and really, it hasn't changed much from those Ancient Greek performances creating catharsis. Zosia Wand describes the feeling of watching great theatre as 'electric', whilst both Adam Quayle and Hannah Tyrrell-Pinder suggest that theatre has to provoke as well as entertain. Many theatre makers will tell how the experience an audience member can have at a performance can be life changing.

Joe Ward Munrow: I've been thinking about what theatre means to me recently and it means everything. Because up until the point I began writing plays, I didn't really have a purpose. I'm not particularly interested in money, all I want to do is write plays and be creative and hopefully earn my living from it. Recently I've become more obsessed with this, so theatre means a lot. Creatively it means a lot, but I think a bad play is the worst experience, it's worse than a bad film or bad stand-up, but a great play is the best experience you can have. The beautiful thing about theatre is that it is so difficult to get right as it is so collaborative: it needs a good writer, a good director, good actors and a good audience. Everything needs to come together for a night of theatre, and then it is just gone, and it is never coming back.

Theatre creates a sense of the communal, a sense of storytelling that can be shared, and storytelling that can be aimed at a certain community or social issue, and therefore still has a relevance to modern society. Looking to new writing, which is what you, the new writer, will be creating, there are many stories to be told within this medium, stories that can be shared in your own community. As Munrow points out above, theatre is ephemeral, there for that one night and then disappearing forever. So what, for the writer, makes this a satisfactory medium to work in? Why does anyone want to write for theatre?

Why write for theatre?

One of the first questions I asked those I interviewed was: why did you want to work in theatre? The range of their answers highlights how personal this choice can be as well as how passionate people are about that choice.

> **Suzanne Bell:** Because it's my home. I could write a PhD about why I want to work in theatre, but it's where I feel at home and I never felt at home anywhere. This is before I thought: oh I want to be a dramaturg or I want to be a director. This is where I feel at home, this is where I feel I have got a place in my life in my world.

> **Lizzie Nunnery:** I always felt really strongly that I wanted to be a writer. I can't remember ever not wanting to be a writer. I was sent to speech and drama lessons when I was still at primary school, I think as a confidence building thing, and what was great about that was reading Shakespeare monologues from when I was a little kid, so it all became quite normal to me. I fell in love with the way language would be used in Shakespeare, and also in the contemporary plays I was introduced to. I was given monologues to read: for example a speech from Roald Dahl or a

John Masefield poem, but then later I might be doing a piece from Brian Friel. At the time it wasn't something I thought about very much, but then when I came to try and write seriously as a student, it felt very natural to me to write scripts. And I was always very attracted to writing dialogue – to exploring tensions between voices, and I found that I could do that quite instinctively. Also I loved the fact that theatre brought together literature and performance, which were two things that I'd separately always been very excited about.

Ruth Little: I didn't set out to work in theatre. It was language and the uses of language that interested me. I studied English literature at University after a brief stint studying to be a vet (surgeons work in theatres too…). I focused on Renaissance literature because I responded to its energy and immediacy, to the sense of new forms of knowledge coming into being (or old forms in new contexts), and then I moved into an exploration of power and powerlessness and the language of scapegoating and demonising, and that led me to drama via classical rhetoric and the early modern witchcraft trials. So it wasn't so much theatre itself as the playing out of social and political relationships in specific and concentrated contexts that interested me. That and movement. I'd also done quite a lot of work as a script editor in film, when I was invited to read plays for the Royal Court. At that stage it was the intense life of the building that interested me. And then I read Caryl Churchill, and saw Sarah Kane's *Blasted*. And then I wanted to work in theatre.

Hannah Tyrrell-Pinder: The moment I can pinpoint it to is the moment I saw a production of *Sweeney Todd* at the National Theatre, and I thought: I want to do that. Initially I didn't know how I wanted to create theatre but I knew I didn't want to be on the stage. Then when I was in my teens I did a bit of directing at school, and I was like, oh yes, this works, I know how to do this, I understand this. And I found it a lot less frustrating than being in a play when I couldn't control what everyone else was doing! From then on, through university, I tried to do as much directing as possible, see as much theatre and read as much about theatre as I could, and I always knew when I graduated I would do something to specialise in theatre, so then I went to Mountview drama school to do a post-graduate directing course.

Chris Thorpe: I didn't really want to work in theatre, I studied theatre by accident. I realised I'd applied for the wrong course when I turned up for the interview at the University in Leeds, and although I'd done a drama GCSE I'd never really thought about working in theatre. But pretty quickly when I got there I realised what was special about it. They were encouraging us to find our own language, find our own way of investigating what it meant to be in a room with other people and the weirdness of that, and I got really, really interested. First in quite a formal conventional way, working through script and putting on plays, but then as we were encouraged to think more about the mechanics and the emotional and political qualities of the relationship between the people in the room, be they audience or performers, and what those labels might mean, I became more and more entranced with the idea that this was something that could be messed about with. [...] the inherent weirdness of the fact that, in a world where we are offered so much in the way of access to information, we still feel it is important to go into a room with other real human beings who may very well fuck it up in front of you. Whether it is explicit or in the act of sitting watching what they do, to have a conversation with others that when it works best, yes can tell you a story, but can fundamentally rewire a little bit about what you think it means to be human – that was a fascination that came very quickly from accidentally going to uni to study theatre. Being given a room and told: just get in there and we will support you to make mistakes for a few years.

Ella Carmen Greenhill: I thought I wanted to be an actor, which is why I did drama at university, but I found I wanted control over what I was doing rather than just expressing someone else's meaning, I wanted to write my own meaning. A friend said: right I'm just going to ring the Everyman and get an application form for you for the Young Writers Scheme. I did all of that half-heartedly, as a defence in a kind of way, and it was so amazing [when I got there] because Suzanne Bell, who ran it at the time, told me I had a style, which was great to hear.

So I thought, maybe I'm alright at this. They were so supportive of my work and that idea of just write whatever you want to write, find what it is you want to write and just do it, and I realised that I found it quite easy to find what that stuff was. I felt I had a lot to say.

Joe Sumsion: I joined the youth theatre when I was 13, and honestly I joined because my friends went there and I knew that you could smoke there without getting into trouble. I had no artistic or dramatic pretensions, but I heard it was a cool place to be. I stayed because I liked organising things, I was a terrible actor, but I liked the project of doing productions, I really enjoyed making shows. I hated doing improvisations, whenever we had to do improvisations I really wanted to curl up, but I really loved putting on shows. Then over time, by the time I was about 16, I thought that I really fancied directing, I liked looking at the bigger picture. Then I did A-level theatre studies, I directed a play during that time, so that was all about me me me. When I left school

I volunteered for Pocket Theatre Cumbria, which was a rural touring company, village halls and community centres around Cumbria, and some theatres, and I loved that. We were a new work company, and I felt proud of the work I did there, making the shows and taking them out to these far flung places in Cumbria, and that's when I got the power of what theatre could be over and above what it meant to me.

Zosia Wand: When I was growing up in South London, around the age of 14, I joined Greenwich Young People's Theatre. It was run from this old church building by a group of theatre in education practitioners, and we devised our own shows, and I absolutely loved it, it just changed my life. Introduced me to different kids and to being creative. I remember one of the tutor directors would write the production every year, and she knew I was interested in writing so she let me write some scenes, and that was the first theatre I ever had produced. I stayed with the group until I was 18. Then I went to university, and the only way you could be involved in theatre at university was to audition for things, and I wasn't interested in that, so I set up a theatre company where we devised our own work, and I wrote the shows out of people's improvisations. So I learned a lot about Mike Leigh and read up on stuff, about community plays, and that led me into working in community arts.

Rob Drummer: From the earliest days at primary school I started being in those shows that everyone does: Christmas nativities; drama as part of the curriculum, so that means storytelling. I went to a Church of England primary school, so the nativity was the first time I can remember stepping onto a stage in front of an audience. I remember, it must have been a dress rehearsal or the equivalent of that, having to be pulled out right at the end and be taken to hospital, for an appointment, and I have asked my mum why this decision was made, but I stayed in costume. I was playing Joseph, and my mum picked me up from school, put me in the back of the car, and I didn't get changed out of this costume. Suddenly I'm on the way to hospital, dressed as Joseph, tea towel and everything on my head, and I have a really clear memory of walking through hospital corridors and people turning and looking, as if to say 'Why is this kid dressed in this strange way?' And at the time I loved that bit of attention and that magic of what it was and what it meant to be dressed up as someone else.

Fin Kennedy: I'm not sure I ever saw it as 'working' in theatre. It wasn't a case of: that's a job, I will go and make my living at it, although obviously I did set my sights on it at some point. I just fell in love with theatre as an art form. I was probably about 11, I began going to youth theatres, and I went to youth theatre for years, obviously that's outside of school, so then I took it as a GCSE option and that leads to A-Level then uni, drama and English at uni, but I never saw it as what am I going to do for a living? I saw it more as I can't not give this a shot because I love it so much. That might sound pretentious, to talk about it in those terms, like it is some sort of calling, but I wouldn't have been a happy human being if I'd gone and done anything else.

Joe Ward Munrow: I didn't really want to work in theatre, I didn't know what I wanted to do; I was a waiter and I was trying to be a stand-up, and then I thought I'd do a TEFL course and go and teach abroad. Then Ella, my partner, went on the Everyman's Young Writers Scheme and she said I should do it the next year. So I did, but rather reluctantly. And then... I loved it! I loved the modern plays we were given, because at university all we were given was kind of Martin Crimp stuff from the 1980s, but on the Young Writers Scheme I realised that you can do anything on stage. Previously I had thought plays were boring, but then I realised it was better than stand-up – because you could make people cry, you could do anything you wanted. It could be intellectual or it could be funny or it could be stupid. So that's why really, because of the freedom of it.

What struck me about these answers was the wide variety of ways people got into theatre and how very un-elitist all of the answers were. There were very few 'Road to Damascus' moments; some people fell into it by accident – as I did – and some people knew that theatre was where they wanted to be from a very early age. Some people know they want to work in theatre, but are not sure in what capacity until they realise that 'control' over the process is something they desire, and that this 'control' comes from being the writer. Through this desire is the realisation that as the writer you have the ability to be creatively daring whilst still reaching out to a variety of communities to tell your stories.

But the bottom line to all of the answers the interviewees gave me is this: I began to create theatre and realised I loved it. And that is my own reason for working in theatre. As Fin Kennedy goes on to say, 'The irony is, it is so hard to make a living at it. I've had my unhappy moments too, even though I do it full time, but the good outweighs the bad, and you find your way through it.'

It does not matter if you went to drama lessons from the age of two or if you began in another career and made a late move to theatre, what is clear is that theatre becomes a passion to those who decide to make a career of it. And that is the first thing to learn from this book: without a passion for the art form, for the medium and for collaboration, it is doubtful that you will ever be able to write for theatre successfully. That is why I have begun with these foundations of what theatre means to those who work in it, for without understanding these foundations, without going out and seeing new plays, experiencing in a communal environment a range of emotions whilst watching a story told and created by a team of actors, designers, writer, director and crew, you will not become a playwright no matter how many exercises on character, form, layout and plot I give you. You have to engage critically and emotionally. Take a look at what may initially seem to be restrictions and work out what you can do with your story to make these restrictions into strengths. Munrow says that you can do anything you want to in theatre, and this is true, but you must understand what those possibilities are, what is viable and what is not, for you to be able to do anything you want. One of the first mistakes new theatre writing students make, I find, is that they try to make a screenplay fit onto the stage. As I shall go on to explore in Chapter 5, there is a lot the playwright can learn from screenwriting, but simply moving a script from screen to stage will rarely work (although interestingly there is currently a spate of theatre adaptations of films and TV shows – proving once again that in theatre, whilst there are rules, there are no rules!). You must experience theatre through scripts, productions, discussion and review, you must immerse yourself in the world. The foundation and established practice of writing for theatre is: loving theatre.

The second question I asked highlights the need for critical engagement. I asked about first theatre experiences, because many of the emerging writers I work with have an idea that playwrights have a very sophisticated view of theatre that comes from a different world to theirs, when in fact, we all have very similar experiences, and not all of them are good! For example, many respondents remembered going to pantos when they were very little:

> **Joe Sumsion:** It was at The Dukes Playhouse in 1973, when I was five, it was a pantomime, *Beauty and The Beast*, and I remember two things about it: I was terrified when the beast came into the audience and looking back in hindsight, I don't know if it was a good fear – I was honestly terrified. And then on the way to the car I pushed my little sister and she banged her head and we had to go to Lancaster Hospital.

I love this story because there is no pretence or faux sophistication. It is a story that will chime with many people. I remember being scared silly of a green witch and hiding under the red velvet and dark wood tip-up seats, screaming until my mum had to pick me up and take me out!

There are also those memories of being in the school play:

Chris Thorpe: I can remember two: one is being in a play at primary, and it was about the plague village, Eyam in Derbyshire, where the vicar persuaded everyone, during the time of the black death, to basically quarantine themselves in the village and die rather than spread it around the locality in what was presented as a heroic act. For some reason we did this play in primary school, and I grew up near Manchester in a place called Lowton, which isn't close to Eyam, but it is a famous story, so we did that show. I played the vicar and I had to do this speech persuading them to not leave the village and die of the plague – which is quite dark for primary school – but I guess there was something about thinking, wow, I get to stand up and pretend to be this dead guy who said all this pretty weird stuff – and it didn't help me understand the black death or the position priests enjoyed or the social or political matrix of the time, but there was definitely something about pretending to be someone who really wasn't me. When I'm on stage now I'm a performer, I'm not an actor, I'm very much myself, but that was my first experience of being someone else.

Then to go to see stuff, we went mostly to see pantomimes, but I remember once, and I can't remember how old I was, going to the Royal Exchange in Manchester to see *The Merchant of Venice* with Tom Conti I think playing Shylock, and I can remember it being really interesting and really great but the main thing I remember is it was a modernised version and you could tell it was a modernised version because Shylock had a fax machine and I just really remember looking at this fax machine thinking, wow, you can have a fax machine in Shakespeare. I guess that was cutting edge technology at the time.

Many people remember the school Shakespeare trip, often loved, more often loathed perhaps, but if you are lucky to get to go to a really good production, it can be a great and life-changing experience:

Zosia Wand: Probably going to see Shakespeare with the school: *Macbeth*. I didn't have a family that were into any form of culture, we were just immigrant, hard-working, no time for that kind of thing. So it will have been *Macbeth* with the school and I absolutely loved it. I knew the play, if we'd not studied the script it would have gone completely over my head, but I loved the witches, and I loved Macbeth and Lady Macbeth, and it was all so dramatic. It was exciting just being in a theatre while it happened, I love the idea that there is a relationship between you and the people on that stage, in that moment, that moment is never going to get repeated, it is different every time.

Rob Drummer: In year nine of high school, just before my family moved back to London from the Isle of Wight, we were taken on a trip to the Barbican to see the RSC production *The Tempest*, down in The Pit and as far as I can remember this was the first high quality professional show that I'd seen, and it was really exciting and accessible, and that play, which is not an easy play, really connected and felt wonderful as a story, and felt relevant, and the language was accessible.

And for many people, apart from pantos, the first theatre experience was with amateur productions. Now, there can often be a snobbery attached to amateur productions, which I feel is totally misplaced. If you live in a small town or have little to no access to bigger theatres, amateur productions can be excellent starting points, both for an audience member and for a first experience working in theatre.

Kevin Dyer: When I was very young I was taken to see a pantomime, it was my first experience of theatre, and I hated it, I just hated it more than anything else in the world. I hated going on the bus with all those other kids, it was like I was packed away by my parents to this thing they thought that children should do. It wasn't until I was at school and I went to see an amateur production *Waiting for Godot* by Samuel Beckett. We weren't a theatre family, after that terrible time with the pantomime my parents gave up on theatre, and we didn't do books in my family, but at school we went to see *Waiting for Godot* and I knew it was totally unlike film, and totally unlike cinema and totally unlike anything I'd seen before, it was just that live experience, and being so close to the actors, that I knew I was up against something very special.

Lizzie Nunnery: I think it was going to see my cousin in an amateur production of *The Sound of Music*. I remember being really interested in the dialogue and the scenes – not really enjoying the songs as music, and getting a bit irritated by the slightly twee melodies, but being very interested in this live event, these real people playing engaging parts. And I had seen little plays in school, but there is something quite different about sitting in a real theatre, in the darkness, with the lights on the performers. It did make me want to be involved in it in some way. As a child I had a confused sense that I wanted to write it and be in it, but I did think it was exciting. And then I saw a production of *Our Country's Good* by Timberlake Wertenbaker at the Everyman when I was in sixth form, so I was probably 17, and I was just blown away by it, and thought it was the most wonderful thing that had ever happened. I was really overwhelmed by the sense of community in the theatre: of people having this intense shared experience, and how well this play communicated huge human issues, and how inevitable it was that we all had to engage with it emotionally. That was when I felt 'this is really what I want to do'.

Ruth Little: I had a friend at school in Sydney whose parents ran an amateur theatre company in their garden shed and I used to weave in and out of that, but without conviction, because there wasn't a strong new writing practice in Australia then, and everything else just seemed like prescriptive make-believe to me. My godfather was a theatre director and composer and I grew up around performers and theatre-makers, though never wanted to be one myself. I think the first professional production I saw was a musical: *Jesus Christ Superstar*, and I saw it in the early 1970s and then I did want to be a performer. Anyone but Christ. Of course I don't remember the productions that bored me, but I do remember seeing Judy Davis in *Miss Julie* by August Strindberg not long out of drama school, and I knew then there was a huge difference between decent and exceptional acting, and the same with playwriting. I was spellbound. And also that language and movement together in a confined and artificial space could have a howling intensity, and that theatre and madness were natural bedfellows.

Of course, for some people that first experience was a major life-changing one. Steven Luckie's story I found particularly inspiring:

Steven Luckie: I can remember my epiphany, my most profound experience, of going to the West End and seeing *The Amen Corner* which was a black production, by James Baldwin, and watching a piece of theatre that was not only staged, profound and creative but actually related to me and my culture. It was a 'wow' moment, like, hang on, there's a group of black people who are doing brilliantly, I have never seen this before, I thought about it, but this is it. Here are these black actors, written by a black writer, and it is well put together and really eloquent and it is saying something, and we're all being moved, and it is so passionate, and it was like: God I needed to see that. Because we can do this. I was in my early teens and I think it reaffirmed itself because it was in the West End, it was like, God, we've arrived. And it wasn't just about watching, it was shining, reflecting back at you. The story is about the South, so maybe the subject matter was coming back and saying something. This was my first visit to the West End, not many people can afford to go often to the West End, and I had bought my own ticket to see the show, I had made that decision. That was it from there onwards.

Finally, for some people, for a variety of reasons, those first theatre experiences were perhaps not the most inspiring in terms of what they went to see, yet they still made a lasting impact on them.

Suzanne Bell: It will have been the Polka theatre in Wimbledon, which we used to go to for school, when I was really little and I don't really remember the theatre or the play but I remember the experience of sitting in the foyer on the carpet having a packed lunch and the coloured walls all painted and the sense of anticipation and excitement before going, and this sense of we're going to share something special and we're going to be told an exciting story, and we're going to have an exciting experience, and it was something special and something different and you weren't in your classroom, and it was kind of like – just that sense, that feeling that made me go wow, this is different and this is special.

Ella Carmen Greenhill: My step-dad took me to see something at Nottingham Playhouse, and I can't remember what it was but it had Susannah from Brookside in it. And I was quite young, I wasn't panto-mime age, but I was probably about 11. I remember being so excited when the lights went down, and that might sound like a really stupid thing to say, but I just sat there, and not knowing what the hell was going on in this play (it was about a guy who was cheating on his girlfriend, I think actually it was probably really sexist and not at all cool) but I was really excited because it was Susannah from Brookside and it felt like a really posh middle-class play. And it finished and my step-dad turned to me and said, 'I'm really sorry, that was a bit shit, wasn't it?' but everyone was clapping, I hadn't really paid attention to the play, but I'd paid attention to the fact that we were all in a room together watching something and the exhilaration of everyone clapping together in the dark, and this is what I remember. So it was an experience more than a play that stayed with me, like, wow, look at this that you can do.

All of these stories highlight something that is very human about theatre: the emotional response it produces in us. Of course other types of writing can inspire an emotional response, but let's go back to that principle of shared experience. It takes a lot of courage for many of us to share something we have thought or felt and have then written down, and yet this is what theatre demands of the playwright. This will be shared amongst not just the cast and creative team but all of those people in the audience, together in collaboration. So to appreciate how theatre makes us feel, and to be able to then be critically aware of that cathartic feeling, that empathy we must have as writers is vital for the creation of good theatre.

As I said at the very start, writing for theatre is different to other types of writing, for very many reasons, and there is no one 'correct' way of creating theatre. I will explore different ideas around making theatre and the more practical aspects in the second part of the book, Speculations, but in terms of establishing practice there are two points I hope these first few chapters make:

1. You are part of a huge worldwide history, dating back to before the fifth century BC.
2. You need to be passionate about theatre as a form of storytelling and you need to be willing to let that passion shine through.

Take these points into the next two chapters, where I will explore what it means to be a playwright as well as the more practical elements of writing a play.

4   Becoming   a   Playwright

In 1934 Dorothea Brande published *Becoming a Writer*. Her aim with this book was to focus on the practice of being a writer rather than produce a series of exercises or useful hints for technique and craft. It is an important and inspirational book, if now rather old-fashioned, that I would recommend to any writer, and in this chapter I am going to shamelessly emulate Brande. Through the insights of the interviewees, I will explore the traits and practice needed to work and create theatre as a playwright.

Brande's contention was that in order to become a writer, you have to be able to think and work like a writer, and this holds as true for playwrights as for any other type of writer. You must understand what qualities it is necessary to foster and what processes help you work or create. One of the best ways to learn this is to hear from those already working in and writing for theatre.

I asked interviewees what qualities they believed to be crucial for a playwright, then collated the answers and ranked them in order of frequency, as follows:

1. Empathy, very closely followed by:
2. Ambition/Drive
3. Humility
4. Knowing your craft
5. Imagination
6. Knowing the business of theatre

I shall explore each of these qualities to see what they mean for the playwright.

Empathy

Empathy is the ability to understand and connect to the emotions and humanity of others. Joe Sumsion suggests that a playwright has to be able to 'capture emotion and human experience as economically as possible with words' whilst Lizzie Nunnery suggests that empathy is about:

Lizzie Nunnery: The ability to bridge the gap and transfer core emotional experiences into other contexts. For example you might not have ever had your life threatened but you have felt fear so you know how to write that moment.

Suzanne Bell also points to empathy 'because my belief is that this is what audiences go to the theatre for, to emotionally engage with something, as well as intellectually, but if you can move them I think it will last a lot longer'. As Hannah Tyrrell-Pinder and Adam Quayle both suggest, it is important to have an interest in people and the world around you, and then translate that into character and story. Fin Kennedy takes this point and moves it forward a little more:

Fin Kennedy: It is so interconnected as an art form, you have to understand psychology, and how people tick, you have to understand society, and culture and different groups, particularly for plays in the modern world. You've got to understand the tradition you are writing in, you've got to have an element of looking slightly into the future, taking the world as you find it and finding the logical outcome of this in the near future.

Being able to understand what makes people 'tick' and to empathise with them is, I would suggest, a quality that is vital to any writer, but the playwright is going to be creating characters that will live through other actual humans, that is actors, in the hope of creating an emotional or even cathartic response in their audience. It is perhaps not surprising, then, that this quality is so popular compared to the more mechanical or craft based practices, because empathy creates character and character creates plot. But this quality is also about being a particular kind of person, the type of person who works like a sponge, constantly soaking up whatever is around them, understanding experience and then being able to translate that in a variety of ways onto the page to see it through into the performance. Empathy, as Nunnery points out, is about being able to extrapolate that experience, to put yourself into the shoes of your character, see the world through their eyes whilst using your own life experience to add veracity to that character's voice.

Ambition/Drive

Ambition or drive came next, although people also used words like tenacity and persistence, which all fall under the same heading.

> **Steven Luckie:** Drive. Drive is over talent. I have met so many talented people who have got no drive and I know they won't go anywhere. [...] It is the hard workers that will uncover, you really have to have drive.

This is a more difficult quality to try and get over to any new writer. Rejection happens. It just does. Even when you see someone feted for their 'first' play in a big theatre, the chances are that this is not their actual first play and that they have written plenty of plays before this. They have simply not given up. Writing is a subjective business. As a playwright you are at the mercy of one or at best two people in a theatre who will read your play and hopefully like it enough to get in touch with you for a chat, whilst probably explaining to you how they cannot produce this play but that they would like to work with you in some way. False pride or shyness has no place here. You have to take all opportunities offered and you have to build on them, and at the same time keep writing and creating new work.

> **Lizzie Nunnery:** Tenacity – the self-discipline that pushes you to keep going with a piece of work. Almost every play becomes difficult and feels like a burden at certain points, and there are times when half of you wants to walk away from it. I read a great book by Haruki Murakami called *What I talk about when I talk about running* in which he compares writing novels to long distance running. Obviously a novel is a long form and possibly requires even more tenacity and self-discipline, but I think it's comparable when you get to draft 15 and people are still giving you notes, and you still know you haven't quite got there yet, but you know you're still reaching for it.

> **Adam Quayle:** Ambition – a lot of time people think you have to write for three or four characters only or it won't be produced. I'd love Box of Tricks to do a season of plays with eight or more characters, because I do believe that we are in danger of getting a generation of writers who are being encouraged to write 'small' plays, which are fantastic, don't get me wrong, but as a director, I have never directed more than five (actors) since 2007.

Both Quayle and Nunnery are talking more about the ambition a writer has for their own work here rather than the drive Luckie talks of, but both versions of ambition are vital to the playwright. The idea of knowing what you want to write and being confident in it, having the drive to push the play forward and believing in yourself as a writer and the piece of work you are creating is an important quality.

Lawrence Till: Inevitably there is the whole thing about persisting. You should work on several things at the same time, not locking yourself into one element, because what if that one element doesn't work? Someone may want that but someone else might want something different, or if you do something and it is successful, you can bet your life someone will want something else, and you can't wait a year to hand over a different piece of work, so spread the work around a bit.

Zosia Wand: You've got to keep going, but pursue the projects you are passionate about, do them for the love of it, and if it is good it will get produced. It is very important to write what you feel passionate about, not what you think other people want.

The words ambition, tenacity and persistence have been used here, but I think these could all be summed up in the term 'self-belief'. Finding a support network, either through fellow students and tutors, family and friends or writing groups, is also a good idea to help you through those times when your ambition and self-belief are waning. I have mentioned throughout this book that writing for theatre is different from other writing because of its collaborative nature. This is true, but perhaps for that first play, or first few plays, you will be writing alone to get the work finished. You may get some development from a dramaturg or a literary department in a theatre; you may have a mentor or be able to workshop the play; but the fact remains that there will be a chunk of time when you will be alone with this idea, when you have to believe in yourself as a writer and be passionate about the work itself to get you through those times when it is just you stuck in a room on a computer, typing. This is when your self-belief may be tested, but be aware that you are not alone in this; it is something all writers feel at one time or another. Be tenacious, have an eye on the end point, and trust in your ambition.

Humility

I mentioned at the start of this book that you may find some of the advice contradictory. This chapter is no exception, because after so many people had pointed to the importance of ambition, persistence and self-belief, the next highest rated quality to come out was humility! Lizzie Nunnery tells a story of her experience after her first big success:

Lizzie Nunnery: I've realised over time that ego can be such a barrier, maybe for all artists, but definitely in theatre. I remember after I'd written

Intemperance that was on at the Liverpool Everyman and was critically well received, and was my first production as a sole writer, having this paralysis. I couldn't write well because there was this expectation on me to write well, and before that point there had been that lovely thing of proving myself to people, of saying 'well you don't know I can do it, but I can'. But when that was reversed, I found that really difficult. I remember I went to a Dennis Kelly workshop and tried explaining this to him: how I was finding it hard to push on with a new project and have confidence in what I was writing, that I was basically undermining myself all the time. He said 'Don't listen to people telling you you're a great writer because you wrote that play. Don't listen to people saying it's a great play. You're not great and you're not crap, you just have to turn up at the page'. I knew exactly what he meant. You can think yourself into all kinds of problems as a writer that are actually nothing to do with the work, nothing to do with what happens on the page or on the stage. They're to do with how you feel about yourself and your image of yourself as a writer. I think the best thing you can do is take each project on its own, work out why you're connected to it, see it through, and like Dennis Kelly says, just turn up at your computer. Even if it's a day when you can't write anything good at all, treat yourself as a professional, as a worker. I think that's key: see yourself as an artist *and* as a worker. This is your craft. It's your job.

There is a fine balance between self-belief or ambition and that overbearing type of ego, where you take no advice and believe everyone who doesn't love your play is wrong. Humility was suggested mostly by the writers I spoke with, rather than dramaturgs and directors, and they suggested that this is a good quality for a playwright because it links to the self-belief aspect. As I mention above, no matter how closely you collaborate with other theatre artists, for every playwright there is always a period when you are working alone on your idea. No one else gets to see these perhaps more lonely moments in a writer's life. We all experience them. But this self-doubt can be an important part of the writer's process, as Joe Ward Munrow and Ella Carmen Greenhill both point out, because it makes you always want to be better, to write the best story you can without letting down the creative team around you. However, you do need to be aware of the 'ego tightrope' you are walking and, as Nunnery suggests, just make sure that you turn up to the page ready to work.

These personal qualities may already be part of you or may be something you learn over time, but the fact that the top answers were about personal rather than practice or craft traits suggests that the emerging playwright needs a good degree of self-awareness. As writers we should all reflect not only on our work but also on ourselves. A meeting with a director or a dramaturg can feel like it has gone wrong, or a rehearsed reading can feel like a total disaster, even first night performances can seem awful sometimes. Understanding how you work emotionally, having empathy not just for others but also for yourself, is an important tool for any writer to acquire, and clearly is in the top three for nearly all those theatre makers I spoke with. Reflecting on your practice, on your own writing process, can also form part of your own critical understanding of your work. Keeping a daily journal, writer's notebook or process log can help you write through ideas and blocks, help you understand what is happening for you emotionally when writing and help you analyse your work in a dramaturgical way. If this sounds scary, it can be, because sometimes as a writer you have to explore what it is inside you that is pushing you forward to write this play about this subject, at this time in your life, and reflecting on your process is vital to that awareness.

Knowing your craft

The next group of qualities all come under the heading of practice or craft traits. A popular theme that runs through a number of interviewees' answers is the necessity to understand the medium you are working in, and this requires several abilities:

> **Joe Sumsion:** To think and write in images. Theatre is a visual form. If you ask people, say what's the best show you've seen, tell us the best moment in it, they hardly ever say 'it's when somebody said...' but they nearly always say 'it's when somebody did...' To think in images and actions.

> **Kevin Dyer:** When I started writing, I wrote some terrible plays. They were terrible because I didn't know how to do it. And when I'd written enough awful plays, I thought it is time I learnt how to do this, so I started thinking about how plays work. You have to know how the medium you are writing in works. What it can do and what it can't do, and especially what it does best. Basically what you have to do is find great stories and write them well. So there are two parts, one is finding the material and two is working out how to tell your story. I believe in narrative, so you have to work out what the narrative is, what the story is, and then you have to do plot. Plot is what writers do to the story to connect it to their audience. Finally, there are three things in a play: character, location and event – and you have to have all three.

As Fin Kennedy says 'you have to know the mechanics – you have to be good at dialogue, understand structure and all that'. Knowing the building blocks acts as a foundation, and this is an area I will explore in the next chapter because it is a vital part of knowing how to write a play. These are elements that can be learned in two ways.

The first is the obvious route of reading craft texts and completing exercises, and there are many good 'how-to' books out there that can help you with this. But this is only a part of the work a playwright needs to do to understand and learn about these building blocks. The second way is to read and experience theatre, as widely as possible. In Chapter 2 I explored, in collaboration with other theatre makers, innovators of the past, and in Chapter 8 I will explore innovators of the present and potentially the future. Looking at the work of these theatre makers, looking at the season your local theatre is putting on and visiting small and large scale theatres will help you become a playwright, because you will begin to engage critically with the work, analysing what it is doing on both an intellectual and an emotional level. Understanding the rules, as Steven Luckie says, is vital.

> **Rob Drummer:** Be an absolute expert in theatre history – this is completely stolen from Tracy Emin. She was judging on a TV show looking for the next generation of young British artists, and in the early rounds of this TV show they had several established artists connecting with these applicants, and this young woman comes in, does something like screws up a piece of paper and puts it on a plinth and Tracy Emin says something wonderful and Tracy Emin-like: she says, 'She's either the most brilliant, wonderful, exciting artist of her generation or she is completely shit.' They talk to this young woman, and Emin asks her what her influences in art history are, and this young woman says something like, 'I don't need to care about art history, I don't need to know anything about the past, I am in the present and I am looking to the future.' And Tracy Emin stops her, and I am paraphrasing this, and says, 'You are completely wrong. You have to be absolutely expert in everything that has gone before you, whether you think it is relevant or not.' And she just exposes this wealth of knowledge and you realise that Tracy Emin is an expert, she knows everything that happened before her, and that is so important for a theatre maker. Whether you reject it, whether you embrace it, you have to understand what went before.

Knowing the history and the tradition of theatre helps you absorb those craft elements, the foundational building blocks needed to write a script, and gives you the space to push your writing further creatively. If you can analyse a play you have read or watched, analyse what that playwright has done that makes a particular aspect work so well, or not work at all, then the practice of critical analysis can be applied to your own writing.

Zosia Wand: You've got to be prepared to interrogate your own work, you've got to be prepared to question everything, go back and turn it inside out if you have to, and be able to discuss your work with someone else in that way, and interrogate it. And keep an open mind about what theatre is and to constantly be learning about what you can do and what you might explore.

So knowing the rules, understanding structure, critically analysing plays, utilising the basic building blocks that form a play and understanding the tradition you are working in, whilst ensuring that you really interrogate the work you create, are all vital craft elements for writing a play. It can often seem that some writers have an innate knowledge of these craft elements, but they can be learned and honed through practice and exercise.

Imagination

Imagination is, I would suggest, impossible to teach, and it is often considered to be the innate part of being a writer.

Fin Kennedy: Probably top of my list would be: be an original thinker. What is the devastating, original thought at the heart of your play, because that's what I want to see as an audience member. You know there is a contract with your audience, which is a bigger, deeper contract than other art forms. Books have a very personal contract, you can pick it up and put it down. TV you can flick it off, go and make a cup of tea, come back. Theatre you have to trek across town, give up your evening, run the gauntlet of public transport and the British weather, pay £25, sit in the dark for two hours to listen to what you have to say – well what have you got to say? It has got to be pretty bloody special. And all the more so if it is a publicly funded or partially publicly funded theatre. Why does this set of ideas in this play justify thousands of pounds of public money and the man-hours? And that is my biggest gripe really with most theatre: it is intellectually thin. Not as thin as telly or film, don't get me wrong, but I don't want to be let down in that contract as a theatre audience member. I want to see the world anew, I want to walk out of that theatre going 'Oh my god, I had no idea that went on, or I never thought about it that way'. And that's the hardest part. You can learn that craft, but if you've got nothing new to say it is kind of pointless.

Does that sound harsh? Well, being a writer can be quite harsh at times, and to succeed you will need to work hard on several different areas all at the same time. It is impossible to try to teach someone to be an original thinker,

but there are some practices you can learn which can help you stimulate
your ideas and imagination.

> **Rob Drummer:** An absolute unquenchable thirst for what our contem-
> porary culture is and seeing yourself as part of contemporary culture.
> That is a broad umbrella for politics and philosophy and sociology and
> diversity and community, and all of these things, and connecting your-
> self to this absolute moment now. Daring yourself to ask the biggest most
> dangerous questions you can. I don't believe it is the sole responsibility of
> female playwrights to put the contemporary female experience on stage,
> I think you might arrive at an interesting play if young men tried to put
> that experience on stage as well. I know lots of young female playwrights
> who refuse to write political plays about the female experience, it doesn't
> interest them.

We, in this country in particular, are living through a period of the most
rapid social change we've seen for a long time. You see notions of family
changing, our relationship to money and Europe, our place in the world
politically, as a global power, conflict and war. We are seeing a city like
London in, I imagine, less than ten years, six out of ten residents will be
of an immigrant background, and I think that as a narrative does not exist
onstage, as it should do. You get on a tube carriage, you get on a bus,
you walk down the road, and the same is true of Leeds, Birmingham and
Manchester to some extent, these communities exist, this diverse sense
of who is making Britain has been changing for several decades. That
dominant culture we are fed, often through TV and often through film, is
so much more diverse than we tend to reflect and I think it is the responsibility of the playwright to understand what that means, and I think here
(at The Bush theatre) in particular I am trying to get writers to respond
honestly and urgently to changing communities. So really plug yourself
in, and have an opinion about this stuff. Whether you are a writer, or a
painter or a photographer, you have to have a pretty solid opinion on a
lot. And my job is both fascinating and exhausting because you pick up
a play about an experience that you do not share, and if it is doing the
right thing, you want to go off and read about that, and you want to go
off and engage with that. So even if you are a writer writing your very
first play, and you have a story to tell, try to resist the temptation to not
look beyond the end of your nose. I think there are a lot of young writers
coming out of university who only want to write about what it means to
be 20, and they've been told that they're brilliant, but I read a lot of those
plays, so let's go a little bit wider than that, let's look a little bit further,
and I think that idea of social responsibility as a writer or as an artist is
really important.

Hearing from someone who reads hundreds of new plays a year is illuminating for a playwright because it gives you a different viewpoint. Writers must never try to write to please a particular theatre, to try and second guess what that director or that literary manager might be looking for, but writing can be an insular process, so hearing from someone like Rob Drummer that the Bush Theatre in London receives many plays a year that all fall into a certain category does give pause for thought: are you pushing yourself enough in terms of subject or theme? By exploring the world politically or through other art forms, such as music, visual art or other texts, the writer can feed their own imagination, become curious about their world. An inquisitive nature then is vital, and goes hand in hand with empathy, as discussed at the top of this chapter. Seeing the world in new ways and experiencing new things in new ways all help to stimulate imagination.

> **Elizabeth Newman:** You need to fundamentally understand story, and I think you can learn story, but I think some people have a gift that they fundamentally understand how to satisfy an audience with a story they want to follow. They understand that they need to create people that the audience wish to follow. And this person has a flaw, something happens to them, the writer should fundamentally understand the dramatic. Also, you need to absolutely love language, because if you love language you will love getting characters to talk, love describing, love using words as weapons. The best writers I know are always reading, because they love words and the world is easier for them through words. That's why a lot of the writers I know socially aren't the best people to socialise with, because words are their way. It's OK not to say it, because they can write it down.

Imagination has to be fed, it cannot come from nothing. Engaging with other art forms and with the world around you will help you in understanding story. Seeing in your own mind's eye how this person, this character you have created, might deal with this obstacle, when all they want to do is pursue their own desire or objective, is key to your imagination and skills in empathetic character creation.

> **Suzanne Bell:** [A playwright needs] curiosity and a constant questioning, and a constant digging deeper and not always taking the easy route or answer for things. A rigour of questions and a rigour of an exploration of life.
>
> Also, imagination. So we may have all felt anger or hatred or jealousy or love or fear or whatever, but if you can show us the truth of that semitone in a new and imaginative way, then it makes us reflect back on our own lives in new ways – and makes us think about our own lives in new ways.

So there was this tiny moment in *Black Watch* by Gregory Burke which had no words to it and was a gesture an actor did around the opening of a letter and missing his loved ones, and the pain of that, and it was a tiny gesture that he did over and over again, made me reflect back on my own experiences of feeling homesick or feeling like I was missing loved ones, and it really stayed with me and I thought they've captured emotional truth in a new way.

This is quite a list, which again may seem daunting, but when you are learning anything new – another language, a musical instrument, painting – you have to begin slowly and build up your skills through practice. Writing is no different. This is why 'how-to' craft books include so many exercises, because writers need to practise. Knowing the type of personal traits you need to foster, knowing that it is not only you who fears rejections or is filled with self-doubt and unable sometimes to bring yourself to the page to work, also helps when becoming a playwright.

Knowing the business of theatre

Finally, quite a few of the interviewees gave some more practical advice about working as a playwright.

Ella Carmen Greenhill suggests that a playwright should go for every opportunity they come across, and make sure they get themselves 'out there, don't be scared to put yourself out there'. And practical advice may seem a little ambitious if you have not yet written your first play, but you can always come back to this section later, when draft 16 is sitting on your desktop, ready to send out!

> **Lawrence Till:** Put value on what you do, because you have to find a way to measure that for your own success, don't wait for someone else to validate you. Because if you do that you may wait a long time, or you might be disappointed because it is not the arena you thought it would happen, or it's not happened as quickly as you want it to happen.

> **Fin Kennedy:** There's also the more career related things, like get a thick skin, get a partner with a job, learn to live cheaply, learn to self-dramaturg so you can cut through the ten different opinions you'll get on your play, meet other writers, drink a lot (but not all the time) and read a lot.

There is a lot of advice in this chapter, and I can understand a new playwright may read this and think 'that is too prescriptive' or perhaps 'yes, that describes me perfectly.' All the advice in this book comes on a take it or leave it basis, as any advice must, but it is often useful to listen to those who are doing it now and this is the very reason I have spoken with so many theatre makers and asked for their tips, their thoughts and their words of wisdom. But if much of this has left you cold or uninterested, then I will leave the final word in this chapter to Chris Thorpe, as I believe this is a piece of advice no one can argue with and yet one that sometimes can be completely overlooked:

Chris Thorpe: Write – that's the prerequisite for calling yourself a writer – write.

5   Building Blocks

Chris Thorpe: If you're writing plays, probably uniquely among the art forms, you're writing an instruction manual because that art will never exist to its fullest potential within the pages of a book or indeed within the mind of a reader, or on the floor of a gallery. That art will only exist with the combined, collaborative efforts of many, many other people. That doesn't mean you have to over-explain things, the difference is you have to be humble enough in the writing of that to realise that other people have to provide the answers – you always need to know what's going on, it is never good enough to say 'oh well someone else will work that out', you always have to have the answers. But you've got to be able to take the fact that other people may have better answers – because what you're writing is an instruction manual, and what the instructions that they think you're giving them are *might* be better than the instructions you think you're giving them.

A theatre script, as Thorpe says, is an instruction manual or it can also be thought of as a blueprint or a map for the creative team. All of the playwright's thoughts, stories and characters are interpreted through this document by a director, actors, designers and technicians, using the instructions given by the playwright; using the dialogue, actions and stage directions. For example, the playwright will never get to say: this is what the character looks like – because the actor may not look like that, for example, or the director may disagree with you, and as the writer, you may well not get a say in the casting anyway.

So as a playwright you need to have the full play acted out and visualised in your head before getting it down on paper through this series of instructions, and then be prepared for a group of other people to take that instruction manual script and create something live that could be entirely different – but potentially better – or could match precisely your initial visualisation. Understanding that what you are writing in a script is not a complete piece of art but is a series of instructions to another group of people is the first building block to put in place.

I touched upon the idea of what theatrical means in the introduction, but I will explore this idea in some more detail here because it can be quite a tricky concept to try and pin down.

Suzanne Bell: [Theatre is] an experience in which the writer, director, actors, designer, everyone, has worked together to tell me something in a way that doesn't forget that I'm here. And I don't mean like breaking the fourth wall, and I don't mean like direct address, but doesn't forget the experience I'm having and doesn't forget that actually what they're doing (in the best possible way) is manipulating the experience I'm having. So, things that did that for me recently have been: *Black Watch* by Gregory Burke, David Harrower's *Blackbird*, and *Port* by Simon Stephens at the Royal Exchange.

Lizzie Nunnery: I think it is about bridging a gap. In a traditional theatre set up there is that essential gap between the stage and the audience, between the performers and the audience. Really great plays often take on that metaphor and investigate how we communicate or how we fail to communicate as humans, how we can and can't understand each other. They ask 'Can we bridge the gap?' I think all plays I consider great do that in some way.

Ruth Little: Unfortunately theatre has too often meant physical discomfort and the frustration of being rendered passive by someone else's completed thought process. And then from time to memorable time it means leaning forward, into the space, as an invited participant, not merely a witness, in the creation and completion of the work. We very often forget that the audience is part of the ecology of a play – as necessary to its meaning as the writer's or director's own intentions.

I often say that writing for theatre is intimate, by which I mean that the writer is sharing the story he or she wants to tell with a group of people who are all in the same room, and by doing so, is bringing this group of people into a world that is not theirs but the playwright's. It is about showing the audience real 'live' characters who will go on to display their desires, hopes, dreams, nightmares, or even entire lives in front of them.

Chris Thorpe: Theatre is a room where human beings meet to look each other in the eye – now with the stuff I do, I try to make that as literal as possible, but it can also be metaphorical, because I'm aware that the actor looking the audience in the eye is not appropriate for certain types of effective theatre. So whether that looking in the eye is metaphorical or not, theatre is a place where people go to look each other in the eye.

Before you begin to write your script, however, you need to be aware of the basic building blocks it takes to create a script. Imagination, as mentioned in the previous chapter, is of course an important tool in any writer's toolkit, but there are some basic craft building blocks that a playwright needs to consider when writing a play.

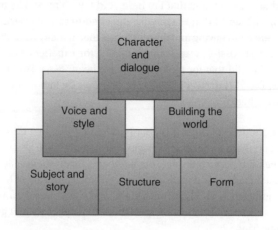

These basic blocks can be organised in any order, but when put together they form the whole, and I will explore each of them in a little more detail now.

Subject and story

What should a play be about? Is it about a family in a living room with French doors opening onto a patio? Is it a whodunnit, a fantasy or a day-to-day story? Is it about royalty or 'common people'? What is a play all about?

Well, it can be about any of these things, and more. You have to go back to that idea of what making theatre means as you make your decision about the story you want to tell. There is the argument that writing for theatre is exactly the same as any other type of writing because in the end you are simply telling a story, just as TV programmes, novels, films and short stories do. But of course the medium you choose to tell the story in impacts on the type of story you choose to tell.

By this I mean that if the story you aim to tell happens completely in the head of the protagonist, it may well be better suited to prose. Or if the story you want to tell is a road trip across Australia, you may want to think about film. But then again, many novels have been adapted for stage and many plays have been adapted for film, so it is never an open and shut case.

> **Ruth Little:** Theatre writing has a charge, which is produced by the inter-play of voice and space, and writers need to know that a theatre work

doesn't begin and end on the page. It comes into being in its relationship with people and place. Theatre writing is less 'innocent' than prose writing because everything in theatre is articulate – brings about change. If it doesn't, it's not theatre writing. The playwright needs to gather a great deal of knowledge – empirical and emotional – about a subject, in order to distil experience in time and space.

The story you tell has to be one that you want your audience to experience live and in a communal space. This means thinking about the things that can only happen in that space, about the relationship between performers and the audience, and what it means for everyone to be together in that room telling or responding to the story. The audience can smell things, perhaps touch things, have eye contact with the performer, none of which can happen in any medium other than live performance. Whilst not specifically the preserve of the writer, there is the lighting and sound, music, off-stage noise and the use of the whole theatre space including the auditorium and bar. So what is it about your story that can utilise these unique aspects?

There is the old adage, 'write what you know', and I think there is some good advice here if it is not taken literally. When you begin to write, having an empathetic understanding of the characters, knowing your plot inside out and knowing your research for the story, will all add to that sense of writing what you know, and ensure you have a firm handle on the story you are telling. And sometimes you are not even aware that you are 'writing what you know'. The first full length play I wrote was about a woman mourning the death of her husband, which I wrote shortly after my father died, during a time when I was re-negotiating a relationship with my mother. And it was only during the read through that I actually realised what I had written. But writing what you know doesn't mean that if you are an undergraduate 18 year old student living in a shared house you have to write a play about a group of undergraduate 18 year old students sharing a house. Neither does looking beyond your own experience mean that a student has to write a play about American gangsters in Detroit just because, although living in the UK, that student has watched a lot of gangster movies or TV series and thinks it might be a laugh to have a crack at that. Parody or pastiche is not looking beyond your own experience. Using your empathy skills to try and understand another point of view, another way of telling a story, is what I mean by looking beyond your own experience, and it might take a degree of reflection for you to understand what it is you are writing, alongside a good deal of research (and not just Internet searches!) to get the story right.

Writing what you know does not have to relate just to what you physically or practically know therefore. Everyone, as I and both Suzanne Bell and

Lizzie Nunnery have already mentioned, feels emotions such as love, hate or remorse, and writing what you know can also mean using empathetic skills to extrapolate from those emotions to create a situation you have personally never experienced, but one you can imagine well through your empathetic abilities. You don't have to write what you know on a day-to-day level, but you can write what you know on an emotional level. Fin Kennedy, when talking about one of his favourite playwrights, puts it like this:

> **Fin Kennedy:** David Greig [...] isn't afraid to tackle subjects massively beyond his own experience, and I'm a great advocate of that. I taught a module at Goldsmiths for many years which asked students to do exactly that. How do you acquire the legitimacy to write beyond your own experience? I find 'write what you know' to be so reductive; write whatever you like as long as you do the proper research, and immerse yourself in that world in some sort of living way rather than just reading a book and doing a bit of Googling.

A play can therefore be about almost anything, but very often it will be a story about a set of characters who aim to achieve a set of objectives.

> **Holly Race Roughan:** I feel like we don't get to exercise our imaginations in everyday life, and theatre acts as a public gymnasium for the imagination. Without the imagination we can't progress as a society or as people, because if we can't imagine a world with racial or sexual equality, how can we progress towards it? So having a space where people can come for a fixed amount of time, where they can exercise their imagination through the suspension of disbelief and through the participation, that's like we're looking after the muscles that allow us to evolve. And I think there are other media that let you do that, especially reading, but I don't think they let you do that in that communal way like theatre does.

This comes back full circle to the idea that theatre means, as both Suzanne Bell and Elizabeth Newman described it, a primal instinct to tell a story to an audience. The communal aspect is important because you can make an audience laugh or cry; you can take them on a journey with you so that they can see the world the way you can see it. And if it seems as if a lot of people who make theatre talk about the bigger social questions, or about politics and their own ideals, then that is the way they see the medium. Theatre can be used as a vehicle for change or as a public forum for debate on the wider social issues of the day, but most importantly, it can also be used to tell 'a bloody good story' as Holly Race Roughan suggests, using that idea of catharsis to ensure an audience has a memorable experience, that they suspend their disbelief, that they go beyond the fact that they are with other people in a room and that these are actors in front of them on a pretend set; and that they emotionally engage with the story that you as the writer chose to tell through this group of actors. All these things are vital to the playwright when choosing the subject or the next story to write about.

> **Lizzie Nunnery:** It's the most liberating and exciting experience as an audience member – more than film or other forms of storytelling. When really great work harnesses the human experience, it humanises us and makes us understand what essentially connects us all.

Whilst thinking about story, it is inevitable that the word plot comes up, and it is trying to understand the difference between story and plot that often confuses new and emerging writers. I think the simplest explanation is that the plot is what you as the writer choose to tell of the story. In other words, the story may be much bigger than the plot. In Chapter 1 I used the example from David Edgar of Sophocles's *Oedipus*, in which Edgar explains how the story has 12 'events'. However, the plot of the play comes in at event nine, revealing the other events through backstory and exposition. This is one of the best ways of explaining the difference between story and plot.

Structure

Plot is also linked to structure, which is another area that can confuse the new writer. Think of structure as scaffolding or framework that holds the play together, that makes sense of the story. Perhaps the best structural form for a new playwright to start with is a linear structure, in which the story goes along a chronological timeline where a series of actions happen that create the plot along a beginning, middle and end structure. So your protagonist has an objective or desire, and in setting out to achieve it, meets obstacles along the way which may or may not be overcome until the end when the situation is resolved by the protagonist either by attaining the objective or not attaining it but learning something profound. Most fairy tales and myths follow this type of structure, as do many novels, films and plays.

Of course, this structure may seem quite prescriptive when laid out like this, especially when there is the argument that there are no rules in theatre, that anything goes. But then again it can seem as if there are lots of rules in theatre, and the playwright must know and understand them in order to break or disrupt them. I always think writing works in a similar way to learning a musical instrument or learning to paint – before you break the rules, you must understand the rules. Once you know how the rules work, you can know how to break them. Aristotle's Unities are a good place to start in terms of structure.

Because the playwright has the audience 'captive' in a space – often quite a small space – for a particular amount of time, trying to write in real time, or in one location, or with continuous action, and by that I mean emotional as well as physical action, is perhaps an obvious and sensible place to start with in your first play. As I have already mentioned, too many emerging playwrights, in my experience, write a screenplay and then try to put it on stage. It will have too many locations, very short scenes, lots of incidental characters and include flashbacks or flashforwards. When I then tell them it isn't a theatre piece, obviously it can be quite disheartening, and they may point out other plays that have short scenes, lots of locations and characters. At this point, I remind them that the writer has to know and understand the rules of theatre first to be able to work out how to break them. For example, two good plays to look at in terms of breaking the rules of a linear timeline are *Betrayal* by Harold Pinter (1978) and *Play With Repeats* by Martin Crimp (1989); *Betrayal* is the story of a love affair but the play runs backwards in time. The audience therefore becomes aware of the secrets revealed only after they have watched a scene where that information is important; it works in the opposite way to dramatic irony, a device used whereby the audience is aware of information and the characters are not – in *Betrayal* the characters are aware of information that the audience is as yet unaware of. But this technique also highlights the unreliable nature of memory, as well as exploring, as the title suggests, how we betray those we love. *Play With Repeats* also disrupts time, but in a much less straightforward way, at one point actually repeating an entire scene, changing only the ending and so highlighting the futility of the protagonist's attempts to change his life. There are many other scripts that play with time, as well as space and character action, and it is part of the creative process to critically understand the way other writers have disrupted the structure of a piece of theatre. If the Unities act as a starting point for your structure, if you limit yourself to the one location, one time and continuous action, you can begin to get to grips with the story you are trying to tell and the characters you are using to tell it. Only then can you experiment with new and perhaps better ways of telling this story, finding ways that will enhance the audience experience.

As the structure is the framework of the play, at some point in your process you will need to write out this framework, most probably in a separate document, so that you can judge whether you are writing the best possible play and whether the events are happening in the best order for the story you are telling to the audience.

Structure can fundamentally change the way an audience experiences your story, and this is where drafting comes in. If you dislike drafting, then writing for theatre may not be for you, because you will probably find that you need to write many drafts before you get to the one you feel you can give over to the creative team to produce.

> **Chris Thorpe:** Accept that 90% of what you write is going be total shit – you need to get out of this magic headspace you think you're in, where the desire to create will automatically produce, in a white hot fire of creation, something perfect the first time. Because that just stops you throwing stuff away.

Now, this again might seem a little harsh, but accepting that the first, second, third, fourth and even fifth draft still needs work is the best thing a playwright can do, and usually this redrafting is necessary because the structure is still not quite right.

Learning how to structure your piece of work, where this building block fits in your writing process, is not a one size fits all type of process. It is useful to hear from playwrights how they work with structure, since they all differ in terms of the point in their process at which they begin to structure and the ways they do this.

> **Lizzie Nunnery:** I try to write the first draft without planning it in too much detail, but then once I've got that first draft out and I've allowed a bit of time to gain some perspective on it, then I'll get quite rigorous with planning. At that stage I write big, extensive plans. For each scene I'll list key events including emotional events, things that need to shift between the characters, lines that have to be said, information that needs to be included etc. I find that really useful because you start to see the play as a puzzle – you start to realise that if the characters are going to talk about something in scene eight you need to decide where to introduce it earlier in the structure. Is it scene two? Also it means that when I'm writing the actual script I've got a blueprint to refer to, so it's easier to make that decision – 'Actually no I'm going to move that bit of information to scene three.' I can shift it around in miniature on the screen and it comes at a point when I've had that creative outpouring, and it needs to get more technical. I find working in that way I throw less away, I'm less likely to write a monologue I've totally got my heart in and then realise there's no place for it in the play.

The idea of seeing the play as a puzzle, as Nunnery suggests, is an interesting one as it means that there are always solutions to the work which the writer just needs to find. This can be helpful if you feel you are stuck at a particular point: think of the structure as a puzzle and work out how to solve it.

> **Fin Kennedy:** For a mainstream play for adults, usually I will start in note form. I am very schematic and I will structure it meticulously before I start, which doesn't mean I will necessarily stick to that structure, but I need to see the play laid out before me before I begin writing. So I tend to write a scene plan in bullet points. Each scene I put onto a new page of A4, in bullet points, and then I print them all out and I stick them to the wall in front of me. And I might move them around, I might add post it notes to add new ideas or new scenes, to experiment with putting that a bit later in the play or a bit earlier, and seeing how it affects things, but I kind of need that bird's eye view of the whole play. I am not one of those organic writers who can just launch into it and see how it goes, although I have every respect for that approach. But partly my approach is a bit of being a control freak but it is also slightly about time management in a writing career. If I just launch into it to see where it went, it would be like going on a journey without a map, I would just end up meandering around and writing a load of waffle that needs to be cut.

Kennedy needs the play to be structured before he begins writing, and this can be done with scene plans and scene-by-scene breakdowns[1] as well as bullet points. One way of working is to get the main bulk of preparatory work done before one line of dialogue is written, and this is very similar to the way many screenwriters for TV and film work. Timelines, character biographies, storylines and scene breakdowns, all of these can help structure your play. Some writers prefer to begin work in a more organic manner, and this is fine too, but at some point in any writer's process structure will need to be taken into account.

> **Joe Ward Munrow:** The first draft – I want it to be fun to do, so I will write the most interesting bits. I write the dramatic bits, the ending, the funny lines, dialogue that I've heard, that sort of thing and it doesn't really make sense in that first draft – it could be 20 pages of snippets. But I work very slowly, I just chip away, I don't force myself to write. So I often write early in the morning and late at night, and it won't be a lot, just a page or something, and I do that for a very long time; I don't structure anything, and I end up with a right mess. Then I get obsessed with structure, and I start trying to move it about and work out what the actual story is – I know the

---

[1] A scene-by-scene breakdown is, quite simply, a list of each scene in order with details, in prose, of what happens, who is in the scene, what has to happen, what the rising action is and occasionally an odd line of very important dialogue.

ending and the start, but I don't know how they are linked, so I create these charts, and I map out where everything is – so at the start I ignore structure completely but by the end I am obsessed with it.

Munrow has a more messy or organic starting point and has to complete this 'first' (or perhaps it would be better termed preliminary) draft before he can begin to structure the play, which then becomes a more planned process. None of these approaches are 'right' or 'correct', they are more to do with writers finding their own way of writing, their own process. Many writers will say that every time they come to a new project, their process will change, but what is vital to recognise here is that the plays have to be worked on in terms of structure at some point. No playwright sits at the blank page and writes Act one Scene one to begin a play. Like many other forms of writing, a play can start out as a mess of ideas or as a bullet point plan or as a full scene by scene breakdown, but at some point structure, plotting and a framework for the story must become part of the process. You can do this through lists, timelines, charts, plans or storyboards, or with a collection of notebooks, whichever way you work best. But remember, each time the process may work a little differently, and that is fine because it means that you as a writer are finding your own way of writing.

Personally, I like to try a different process each time. Sometimes I will write out a logline that sums up the idea in one sentence followed by a full prose synopsis and then a scene by scene breakdown before making a first draft. Other times I will write 'chat' until I know who the characters are, what their stories are and where they are going in the plot. Then I can begin to structure.

> **Billy Cowan:** I walk about with the idea in my head for a while, develop-ing it, playing with it, seeing if it can go anywhere. When I'm sure the idea can become a play, I write down a scene by scene breakdown of the story. I then do character back stories for the main characters and then I start writing the dialogue. Sometimes problems happen at the scene by scene breakdown stage when I can't 'see' the whole story. When this happens I do the character back stories and then just start writing in the hope that the story will reveal itself organically. If I can't get a scene by scene break-down though it's usually a sign that there's something problematic with the idea and I may have to ditch it.

For Cowan much of the preliminary process, the 'pre-writing' process as Amanda Boulter (2007) calls it, happens through thinking the idea through so that if he cannot see the whole play in his head by the time he starts the structuring process, he is aware that the piece may not work at all. Nunnery has yet another different approach, but what is clear from just these few examples is that however the process works for the writers, they begin in a similar place, in that there are fragments, characters and ideas which can then be structured to create the whole story:

> **Lizzie Nunnery:** I start by writing an awful lot of notes. They will be a mixture of freeform ideas about themes; chunks of dialogue, monologues – just letting characters talk; bits of planning, outlining what will happen in each scene and starting to outline plot. All of that can occur in quite a haphazard way.

> At the same time I will probably be reading. Depending on what sort of play it is, I might be reading different sorts of things. With *The Swallowing Dark* which was about asylum I read a large amount of news articles, but also websites, like the UK border agency website, getting an understanding of legislation and statistics. I felt that if I was going to write it I needed to really know my stuff.

> But also I'll read play texts. I do find it useful to have core play texts that I go back to, that remind me of what's possible, of what I want to do. They might change between different plays I'm working on. When I was working on a commission for Druid Theatre Company in Ireland the Literary Manager there said to me quite early on that I should read *Copenhagen* by Michael Frayn. While I was writing, I read and re-read that play, and every time that I felt I had no idea what I was doing with my own play I'd go back to that script. It wasn't a matter of writing a play in the same style, or even using the same content or themes. It was about the confidence of form: someone taking on a story in this very bold theatrical way that dealt with real events and characters who are dead in the present of the play. That was the thing I was grappling with and getting anxious about, and every time I went back to that Michael Frayn play, I thought 'This is completely possible, and he's done it so confidently and boldly and I can do that too'.

Nunnery's process includes reading other plays, highlighting the importance of knowing other work rather than believing that when you are writing something it is better for you not to read or even see other plays in case you wander off track or are overly influenced. If you know that as a writer you have the propensity to be over influenced, then perhaps reading one particular play would not be a useful. However, perhaps reading a range of plays by different writers might be included in your process. What is important is to recognise and enjoy your process and see it as a form of continuous creative exploration.

Kevin Dyer: What I do is I try work out what the story is, in plot terms and event terms, and I try to find out what the story is about, what's the big driving engine underneath it. And then I storyboard it.

I think it was FR Leavis who said a story is a series of events in their time sequence, so I try to work out the series of events in their time sequence. This happens and then this happens and then this happens and then this happens – that's how all stories work. Once I've got that, I can then work out how I'm going to tell it. I find it really useful to know the timeline.

And that phrase of Dyer's – how I am going to tell the story – is the most important craft element of being a writer. Finding the best way to tell the story may involve finding different characters, experimenting with different starting points, finding the inciting incident and seeing where the chain of events following that incident will take you. Immersing yourself in the world of your play is important and helps with the structure, because you want to spend time with those characters, with that story, and you want to play around with ideas – what happens if I do move this event from Scene 8 to Scene 3, for example? Of course, you want your audience to be able to follow your story, but also the audience should be able to work with the story: remember what it is that will make your script theatrical, go back to those definitions of what 'theatrical' means so that you know this script could not be for any other medium.

Another really useful thing to do if you want to explore and understand structure more is to look at screenwriting craft books. Some of my favourites include Snyder *Save The Cat* (2005), Syd Field (2005), Robert McKee (1999) and Craig Batty (2008, 2012), Dancyger and Rush (2013) and Vogler (2007) although there are many others. Whilst it should be recognised that there is a marked difference between writing for screen and writing for theatre, knowing how screenplay structure works can be another useful tool for the playwright, because, perhaps in very basic terms, screen tends to prioritise story and therefore the advice given to screenwriters on structure can be very useful to look at.

Ella Carmen Greenhill: I've been doing a lot of TV stuff recently, where the first 10 minutes could almost be a play in its own right. All of last week I was immersed in the fast pace of TV writing, and I think the main difference is the prevalence of story, and often fast-paced, slightly clichéd story, which is frowned upon in theatre. It is not good theatre writing but it is the opposite in TV, you can't have anything too subtle. For example two people talking in a room can be really intense on stage, but for TV that's not interesting at all. There's a common misconception that

writing for theatre and writing for TV go hand in hand; I think it is difficult to do both, because they are massively different. I was amazed when
I first found out about storyliners for continuous drama, so writers are
literally just filling in the spaces.

Screenwriting is another form of collaborative script writing, but because
more people are involved in the story structuring process – storyliners, script
editors and producers for example – structure becomes much more prominent, and there is more specificity around acts, scenes, ABC storylines, for
example. Often writers new to theatre also want to understand how acts
and scenes work, because this is how Shakespeare and other canonical
playwrights structured their plays, and new writers are often aware of the
prominence of acts and scenes in screenwriting craft texts. Acts and scenes
are not necessarily what we mean by structure, although understanding
what they are can be helpful when learning to structure a play.

Acts are the largest division of the play, and often correlate to the idea
that a story has a beginning, a middle and an end, or in other words, a set-
up with an inciting incident, the action and complications, and the resolution. In each act there are scenes which indicate a change of character
focus, time or place, and the rising action towards the climax or resolution
increases through each scene. Few modern plays retain the use of acts;
scenes are the more often used unit of action, although again some playwrights prefer to use the act as a division. As ever, there are no right and
wrong answers.

The concept of scenes can cause confusion for new writers. When, for
example, do you move onto a new scene? Put simply, most scenes change if
time, location, action or character demands it, and this is why the scene is
the main unit of action for a play.

These units are useful for structure whilst not actually being the structure. For example, a first draft of a play may have ten scenes but the
final draft ends up with two, or vice versa, depending on how the writer
decides to structure the plot to tell the audience this story. There should
always be that sense of rising action through a scene however, the sense
that the story is moving towards the resolution through a series of complications and incidents, which the audience will in some way find satisfying and be able to work with when everyone is together in that room
watching the play.

> **Billy Cowan:** There's more restrictions, limitations to what you can
> achieve (in theatre). You need to create within the parameters of physical
> space and time and you have to learn how to make these parameters your
> friends instead of enemies.

Many emerging playwrights can get frustrated with what they perceive to be the restrictive parameters of theatre, longing for what appears to be the relative freedom of screenwriting. But as Elizabeth Newman points out, 'There is more freedom in theatre, because the form is freer, the parameters are freer'. This may seem as if I am being contrary here, deliberately choosing two opposing viewpoints, but both Cowan and Newman make an important, and actually quite similar, point. Theatre may at first seem to be very restrictive, and this is what Cowan is referring to, because you cannot have lots of locations and lots of actors (although of course you can still have lots of characters) so what the playwright must do is, as Cowan says, embrace these restrictions and learn how to use them to tell the story you want to tell, and once you can do this then, as Newman says, as a writer you become freer, feeling as if there are no boundaries, because theatre can show whatever you want to show on that stage, as I shall explore further in Part 2.

When you begin writing your first play, reflecting on your poetics as a writer, on your philosophy of writing, is important for your creative development. You not only need to interrogate the work, but also the way you write, because there are as many processes as there are writers.

> **Chris Thorpe:** Decide on the question you are asking, about who we are and why we do what we do, put that question to yourself in the simplest terms, research possible responses to that question, and you can be very tangential about that in terms of anecdotal stories, in terms of historical events, in terms of the way that's been put in art before, in terms of news and current events, in terms of imagined meetings between types of people and find a first line, not necessarily a form, and just write from there. And the form will not necessarily flow from the first thing you write – you might write a dialogue scene set in a minutely described place and that will in no way resemble what you eventually come up with, you might write a ten page monologue without any punctuation and that will in no way represent the dialogue you eventually come out with – but just find your first line and write. And it'll be the image or first line that drops into your head and resonates, and there is an almost perceptible clang when it hits the kind of empty bottom of my brain.

Form

Form, linked to structure, is often another difficult concept to pin down, but the basic definition of form is the way that you use the theatricality of the piece and how you choose to tell the story in a theatrical way. So, it may be a linear narrative, it may be interrupted time, you may choose to use monologues only, you may choose to make this a multimedia piece, use a chorus, use one or two actors playing many parts. You may choose to disrupt all the usual forms of theatre, as Caryl Churchill does in *Seven Jewish Children* (2009) or *Love and Information* (2012) where she takes a theme and writes a series of episodic scenes that can be played in any order. However, to do this you have to be familiar with the standard forms of theatre. Again, knowledge of the Unities comes in handy here, as does the idea we keep returning to, that if you want to change the way you write theatre, if you want to disrupt traditional theatre, then you have to have a very firm understanding of what it is you are disrupting. Perhaps the best way to look at form is to explore some examples.

> **Fin Kennedy:** There are people who are pushing the boundaries of the art form, some examples would be Katie Mitchell and Caryl Churchill and Martin Crimp. You can make that case in an academic sense or in the sense of whose work moves you and whose work speaks to you. For example with Katie Mitchell's and Caryl Churchill's approaches, I'm very glad they're happening, but their work leaves me a bit cold, if I'm honest. Less so Martin Crimp, I was a big fan of his for a time. I thought *Play With Repeats* was a brilliant use of structure and *Attempts On Her Life* famously, it sort of showed us there was another way. And that is really important when that happens.

> My personal favourite is David Greig [...] And although Greig is not known for playing with form, *The Strange Undoing of Prudencia Hart*, which I saw in Edinburgh (where you got a free whisky with your ticket) uses the music hall tradition and it was a proper good night out; the band were the actors, and it was a brilliant sort of wintery tale. It is about this Scottish academic who specialises in folktales and goes off to the highlands to research them, gets snowed in in this village, is locked out of this pub, ends up being out all night in the snow and meets this guy who turns out to be the devil and so she gets caught in a folktale of her own. There is a lightness of touch and a traditional spirit of telling you a ripping good yarn here. His most recent one was really innovative: *The Event* was reported as being inspired by the Norway shootings, and he really kicked against this, as it was not entirely fair. It was set among a multicultural community choir who are set upon by this gunman and it is about the aftermath of that, and about their attempts to heal themselves. It was done with two actors and a community choir, one of which was the choir leader and the male actor played all the other parts, but there was a real community choir from whatever town they were playing in. The choir had scripts, and they just read in the lines opposite the actors – they had rehearsed the

songs – and the play follows the story of the choir leader and her attempts to understand why someone would do that. It was inspired in the way that it had such a rawness because of the nature of these untrained actors on stage from the community choir, and in a play about damaged humanity, it was the most inspired innovative decision.

So form is about the way you choose to tell the story and the devices you use to create that emotional response from the audience and these need to work with the story you are telling. This idea can link back to those innovators I explored earlier, for example, and you may decide that you want to write in an epic or naturalistic form because that best suits your story. Form can influence how you create characters, where the piece might be performed, how you use the language and dialogue in the piece.

Suzanne Bell: If fundamentally you work around there are only seven stories ever told and retold, so how are you telling this story in a way that hasn't been told before? What's the truth in that that hasn't been exposed before? What's your truth for that story?

Ask of every project, why am I telling this story now, why am I writing this play, why is it me and not someone else, who am I to this story, why has this story come into my head and won't leave my head alone? And what is the experience I want the audience to have and how can I convey that on the page. If you look at the Tasmanian playwright Tom Holloway or the American playwright Dan Lefranc, the way they lay their work out on the page is an expression for them of the experience the audience will have, it is imbued in everything they do. I think Duncan Macmillan does this too, the form of the play is part of what they do.

So whilst the story you are telling is vital to the success of the play, the form you choose to use is potentially as important, but crucially, not at the expense of the story. There is little point in starting a playwriting process with the idea of form if there is no story to tell.

Elizabeth Newman: I spend a lot of my time reading plays that are writers playing with form but not understanding the fundamentals or the basics. When Martin Crimp played with the fundamentals with *Attempts On Her Life*, he had got it by that point, and I feel like we're not making the Look Back In Angers or the All My Sons – those plays are not being written any more, but they are great plays with people having life-changing conversations, which audiences are interested in going to see. Writers can't keep going, well no one wants to produce my play because they say

it won't sell any tickets. If you write a good story, we will know if our audience wants to come and see it. Writers have to know that we as theatres
are not stupid. If we read a great story and we know our audience will
love that story. If you are the next Arthur Miller, we ain't going to say 'No'.
What we're not going to do is take a punt on somebody who wants to set
aflame five posts on stage and do the Hakka, and challenge the form of
storytelling, when we don't have enough money to do that and we know
our audience are not going to enjoy it. And we're not pre-judging our
audience, saying they aren't bright enough, no, no, no, no, no. Since the
beginning of time people have loved a beginning, middle and end with
people at the heart of an adventure. There are certain things in life which
are fundamental, and storytelling relates to life, it is experiential, which is
why theatre involves sound and seeing, because it is how we experience
life. I get slightly frustrated when theatre makers and writers go, well this
is just because everyone is narrow-minded and stupid and won't get my
work – and I go, OR we have all clocked onto something you haven't yet,
that fundamentally we want to understand why we exist.

Form can be the way the text looks on the page, the style you choose to
write in and it will also include your voice. Experimentation is key, and
workshopping the play with actors or getting it read aloud will help with
this, as will some good dramaturgical script development, because it will
be through this work that you as the writer will be able to tell if the story is
coming across to the audience in the way you want it to. The form will also
be linked to the relationship the play has with the audience. In Kennedy's
David Greig example, the audience felt as if they were almost part of the
action, they were given a drink in their ticket price and they felt included in
the narrative, in the storytelling.

Theatre, shared experience and catharsis can be created through mime,
music, dance and clowning as well as through beautiful or poetic language,
and because it is so literally three dimensional, the playwright has options
that perhaps no other writer has.

The form you choose to write in may be different for each story you tell,
or you may find a particular form that suits you. However, be aware that
the form you choose can greatly affect audience reception of your play.
Form becomes an integral building block, although one you may not
immediately think of, when dialogue and character seem to be the most
important aspects of writing a play. But it is vital because the form needs
to work with both the story and your purposes in telling that story. So, as
a very basic example, if you choose a very naturalistic form for a super-
natural or a macabre story, then you heighten the sense of the uncanny

because of the form you are choosing to tell the story in. Using comedy to make a serious point is a choice of form, as I mentioned in Chapter 2 when discussing the work of satirical writer Joe Orton, for example. One of the best ways to learn about form is, of course, reading and seeing as many plays as possible, then writing in your journal the effect that play had on you and analysing what it was that created this effect, not just the story, the characters and the dialogue, but also how the story was told to you and the audience around you.

Voice and style

Many students say to me: if we are writing for a collaborative theatre experience where actors will say my words and a director will tell the actors how to say them, how can my voice still come through? Whilst that may be a simplistic way of looking at the creative process of producing a piece of theatre, I find that a valid question – of course it is a question of defining what is meant by a 'playwright's voice'. Even though you will be creating characters and writing solely through their 'voices' in terms of using dialogue (and of course action), the writer's voice will always come through in terms of your writing style, what the story is that you want to tell, how you want to tell it and what questions you intend to ask. Even if writers believe that each play created is totally different, looking back over old work it is often clear that similar themes, ways of writing dialogue and character choices are repeated, even if you think you have written something totally different in your latest piece.

As discussed in the previous chapter, empathy as a trait for the playwright is vital and this links strongly to the idea of voice.

> **Elizabeth Newman:** Empathy, in a similar way to actors, is one of the key things for a playwright, that someone can imagine themselves in a different situation, being different people with different voices but still retain the authorial voice. And also through empathising, wanting to connect to the audience [...] Eugenio Barba came and taught my directing class, with a translator – and I said to him: I only want to make political work, I am a political being (bless my soul for being so annoying!) what would you recommend to someone who wants to make political drama? He laughed and he said: you don't need to make political drama because you are your politics, and if you are completely secure in what you believe, know, think and understand about the world but remain inquisitive, your beliefs will excrete through your work.

An authorial voice is about you knowing what you believe, and without any shadow of a doubt, that will come through. I don't mean authorial voice in the way that, for example, Simon Stephen's plays always have a similar kind of rhythm or pace, I mean an authorial voice like Timberlake Wertenbaker or Edward Bond, which do have similarities in the way they put things, from play to play, but that is because what they believe hasn't changed. And you can't change who you are – you can speak through other characters through your empathy for them, but your beliefs won't change.

So your own voice will come through in two ways: in your style and in your beliefs or what you choose to write about.

Rob Drummer: Your voice is what you have to say. Ask yourself what is your position on this, and then think about how you are going to express that position. You have to carve out a space for thinking time, to think what is the only narrative I can tell now?

You will already have a voice – you may not believe that you do, but you do – and it may take time, a lot of writing and a lot of reflecting to recognise what your voice is, even though it may be entirely clear to others reading your work. The most important thing to remember is not to try to copy other writers' voices. This may happen in the early days of being a playwright when you may feel an influence very strongly – I remember I certainly did with Pinter when I first started writing. But over time you will write through this, discover your own style and your own outlook on the world you want to write about.

To a certain extent, voice and style may seem almost interchangeable for the playwright, but in the same way a playwright can play with form, they can also play with the style of the piece. Some definitions might tell you that style is about naturalism, realism, epic theatre, some of the styles of the innovators I explored in Chapter 2. Style can be linked to a particular theatre movement, which is therefore linked to a particular historic moment in time or a particular socio-political situation.

Style may also be defined in terms of the whole theatre production, but can be mixed up here with form to a certain extent. This is why for me the idea of 'style' is strongly linked to the writer's voice. As a playwright you are working at a particular moment in social history, in a particular country and culture, and the style you write in will be as influenced by this as it will be influenced by your own voice. The difference I would suggest is that your voice is innate in you, whereas style can be explored and learned as a craft technique if it is not innate.

Recognising that your work might fit a certain style, a certain type of theatre, may take some experience, but again being aware of the cultural world around you can only help you, the emerging playwright, find your own voice and the style you want to work in.

Building the world

This might seem a rather unusual building block, but what I am talking about here is not building a world as you might for a fantasy or sci-fi novel, although there are certain parallels. Building the world of your play is an important part of the process, because everyone in the room – creative team and audience – is aware that what they are part of during that performance *is not real*. Therefore, because the audience and creative team will buy into the world you have created, you need to know that world really, really well.[2]

Again, it is about thinking what you can do with this world you are creating on stage. Think about the things that can only happen in this medium.

> **Kevin Dyer:** One of the things I like to do is use food, real food, cooking food, smells of food, because I know no other narrative medium can do that.

Using food, for example, a world can be created in which a middle-aged couple who are bored to death with each other use meal times as the only point of connection, a private time when no one else can see them – but the audience can. Or the couple out on a first date eating aphrodisiac types of food thinking no one else can see them – but the audience can. Or the mother in the kitchen who spends her whole life cooking for a family who never come in to see her – but the audience can.

The world you create may have an appearance of reality, but it is not reality. It may not relate to any form of reality we know, but the characters must act as if it is the only reality they have ever known. The audience and the theatre maker make a bargain to step into and accept this world, in person. And that is crucial. Whilst novels and films or TV shows might also make a similar bargain, only theatre makes this bargain face to face. This means that the playwright has to understand every aspect of the world they have created. The world has to have a solid foundation and rules you understand,

---

[2] To explore further you might want to do an internet search for the Elinor Fuchs article *EF's Visit To A Small Planet: Some Questions To Ask A Play.*

that you will not break. The rules have to have a reason, if not a logic, and the whole world has to work within these rules.

This is not about the look of the world – that will come down to the designer – but it is about how the world works, and that is something only the playwright can decide.

Character and dialogue

The last two areas in terms of building blocks are character and dialogue. These may seem the most important to discuss in regard to a play, and on a certain level, I agree because, as all creative writing handbooks will tell you, character is story, and theatre writing is no different. You will need to have a protagonist, possibly an antagonist, and you will be telling their stories.

Character will form the basis of your play because every story starts with the idea: it is about someone who... Your character will face obstacles to reach their goal, will overcome these obstacles, or indeed may not, and their journey arc will take them to some sort of resolution, which does not necessarily mean a happy-ever-after type of ending. This means though that the whole play hangs on the central characters, who will begin the play setting out to answer the main question of the plot and will then move forward to the endpoint, where the central characters are offered some form of answer.

> **Zosia Wand:** I allow myself to sit down and write a load of old rubbish. That's the first thing, to get something down on paper. And it will probably be dreadful, but if you were a potter and you threw a lump of clay down on the table, you wouldn't expect it to look like a pot immediately. You need your raw material, and until you've got that down, you don't really know what you're writing about. So I allow myself to write a first awful draft and then to interrogate it. Ask questions, see what patterns are in there. Then I like to develop the characters, spend a lot of time with the characters and get to know them really well. I won't know them well enough until I have written several drafts. I know that I know my characters well enough when they start talking to me when I'm not working on the play. I find that the first draft is about turning your head inside out and I hate it. And I absolutely love it when you get to the bit where the characters are like real people that you know. And you can put them in any situation and you'd know exactly what they'd do. That's why I also like to recycle characters. Think of them a few years on, change their names, stick them in a new place and see what happens. When I'm writing a first draft of a new script and I get a bit stuck, I'll sometimes put a character

from a different play in it. It raises the bar then because the other characters have to be developed to that level.

There are exercises in Chapter 6 which you can use to explore character, but again, in a similar way to the work you need to do on structure, there will be work you do on the characters outside of working on the actual script, and this can happen in a variety of ways.

> **Kevin Dyer:** I have to work out the arc of every character, what they want at the beginning, and what they get at the end. And I work out for each character their journey through time. And there is nothing very genius-y about that, it is quite craft based. But I have seen so many plays that don't have endings or have terrible endings because the writer hasn't worked out the ending, so I work really hard to sort everything out and make sure it leads up to that ending. Because I think that if I can get all those practical, nuts and bolts, structural things right, it frees me up to write creatively.

All the building blocks, the nuts and bolts in Dyer's term, explored in this chapter are intimately linked – form, plot, character, style, dialogue, world, structure, story. They overlap and affect one another but at some point in your process you will need to concentrate on each block individually, to ensure that they are all working together to bring the whole together.

New writers to theatre often say to me: 'I'm no good at writing plays because I can't write dialogue'. But dialogue is simply another tool to tell the story you want your characters to tell; being a good storyteller is important for a playwright, good dialogue technique can be learned. As Joe Ward Munrow says, 'it is just a stage, and words and you can do whatever you want within those confines', and that simplicity is important. You explore the story and the character through the words and you can do whatever you like within that space. There are ways of improving dialogue through writing exercises, but also listening to people, how they talk, different ways of speaking, accents, idioms and local word usage, alongside knowing the story and the structure of the play solidly and knowing what the characters have to say to get you from plot point A to plot point B.

One exercise I like to send student writers out on is to eavesdrop in public places and to try and note the way people speak, listen to how they hold conversations, what those conversations reveal about their relationship and their status within that relationship, how they flirt, berate, challenge, discuss, negotiate. Who we are speaking to, and why we are speaking to them, influences tone, language use and degrees of familiarity. The devising process is another useful tool in terms of being able to listen to actors

improvise and getting those speech rhythms for dialogue in a play, something which can be done in a workshop process, even after the first one or
two drafts, or before you have even begun to write.

As dialogue is your main tool, you must ensure that each line you write
serves a purpose. The actions of the play, and by this I mean the emotional
actions of the characters not physical actions, the actions they are feeling
that impel them to the course of action the plot is taking them along, come
through the dialogue. Of course, in a first draft you might write quite a lot
of 'chat' to get into the story and the minds of the characters, but when you
redraft you have to be ruthless. Think about dialogue as a row of standing
dominoes, to use David Ball's analogy from *Backwards and Forwards*. Once
you hit that first domino, and it topples hitting the next, which topples and
hits the next and so on, it is impossible to stop all the dominoes toppling.
This should be how dialogue works. One line hits the next, which hits the
next, in a way that seems inevitable for the characters and the story, and in
a way that ensures the action rises to the climax of the piece.

To improve dialogue you must learn to really love language, which is a
heart instruction, and to learn how to control your use of exposition or the
telling of backstory, which is a head instruction. If you find dialogue difficult, reading and watching plays, alongside various exercises, can help you
hone these skills.

This chapter is perhaps the longest of all in the book, and has covered the
basic building blocks, all of which must be put together in whatever order
suits your writing process best. This is the theory, and in Chapter 6 we will
further explore these blocks creatively through a series of exercises that I
have used in teaching and that some of the interviewees use in their own
practice and process.

6 Foundational Exercises and Key Points

Exercises are an important part of the writer's process. No new piece of writing is 'good' or 'great' in its first draft form and all writers get stuck sometimes. Writers, like any other type of artist, need to practise. Great musicians practise their guitar, piano or saxophone every day. Great artists may pencil sketch the subject of their next painting or sculpture many times and from many different angles, or use photography or video to capture those likenesses before they launch into the work itself. And writing is no different. The playwright must practise writing, alongside critical reading of novels and poems and watching plays, TV shows and films, before launching into that first draft.

The following exercises come from a long tradition of writing exercises, and you may well have seen similar ones before, so again please just work through those that are useful to you. Some are aimed at those who are writing their first play, some are merely 'playing' exercises. Some are to be done when working alone, some can be completed in groups or in collaboration.

Exercise 1: Starting point (for sole or group work – most useful for an actual play)

It is perhaps more usual to see this sort of exercise in a book on screenwriting, but I do think it can also be very useful for playwrights to try to get into this discipline: write a one sentence pitch or logline for your play idea. And by this, I am not referring to the slogans you see on film posters and not necessarily those famous high concept pitch lines, for example: 'High Noon in Space', although there is a lot to be said for them! But for the playwright, it is important to try to encompass your whole idea in one simple sentence before you even start to write one word of dialogue or one bullet point of structure. For example, for the play I co-wrote with Paul Hine, *Project XXX*, a play about the mainstreaming of internet pornography in young people's culture, we started the whole project with the following line:

What if, when Romeo met Juliet, he was already addicted to Internet porn and wanted to film their first time, uploading it for the whole world to see?

Now, the story changed quite dramatically from this over the writing process, but the concept that we were exploring, of an 'old-fashioned' story of young love against the backdrop of the digital world, remained a useful anchoring point for us during the writing process; as both of us were apt to wander off on flights of fancy every now and then, the other could bring the logline out and we came back to what it was we were trying to say, what question we were asking of the audience.

So, take your idea for a script, be it short, one act or full length, and try to capture the theme, the plot, the characters in one line, hopefully creating the question you are wanting the play to ask the audience.

> **Lizzie Nunnery:** I like to know what I'm writing about and I try to get it down to one sentence which is usually a question. I then pin that sentence to the top of my laptop and use it to anchor me through writing a play. It's something Suzanne Bell taught me in the Young Writers Programme at the Liverpool Everyman and Playhouse 10 years ago and it was a great piece of advice. For my play *Intemperance* the question was 'What does poverty mean?' For *The Swallowing Dark* it was 'Can we ever tell the truth about ourselves?'

You can of course take plays you know well (or TV or film dramas) and see if you can create one-line pitches or questions for these as well, purely as practice.

Exercise 2: Character (for sole or group work – most useful on an actual project or play)

Character is clearly vital for any piece of creative writing. Knowing your characters inside out will propel your story forward and form your plot. And there are many great character exercises out there, in many creative writing craft or 'how-to' books. These might include exercises such as listing your characters' hopes, fears and desires, what they may have in their shopping trolley in the supermarket (or online), what is in their music collection, on their bookshelf, in their box sets, who their favourite people are, listing the characters' memories, what other people think of them, what they think of themselves, their favourite food, favourite colour, etc. But one way of thinking about character that I find really useful is to split the character timeline into three:

1. what they were born into (gender, ethnicity, parents, class etc)
2. what they have become through the culture in which they were brought up (schooling, location, family members and position, friends, hobbies)

3. what they are like at the point we meet them in the play (job, relationship, fears, desires and dreams, class, habitat)

Splitting your character timeline into three is helpful when building character as there are some things about your character which should be unchangeable (first category) and then things you can change as the character progresses through his/her story arc (third category) but which you will always have to find the root of in either the first or the second category.

Exercise 3: Character (sole work – can be used just as an exercise or on an actual project or play)

Another way into character is to find the character's voice, and this can be done through monologues. It is something many writers do, and something I encourage all my students to do.

> **Ella Carmen Greenhill:** I like to write monologues of characters as a way of getting to know them, that rarely make it into the play – you can make them a bit rubbish because you know they will never go into the play but you can get it all out.

The important point to underline here is that these monologues, as Greenhill stresses, will more than likely never make it into the play itself. The monologue is simply a route into getting to know your character, hearing that voice and letting yourself be surprised by where your character takes you. As Greenhill goes on to say:

> For theatre work it is really important to not know some stuff, to try and keep the excitement going. Chris Thorpe said once 'my character just took a dead bird out of his pocket, I didn't know it was in there.'

You can also advance this by writing conversations or 'chat' between your characters, again always being aware that this work may never end up in even the first draft; this is just exercising your character writing muscles.

Exercise 4: Plotting and story (sole or group work – creative exercise – but the process can be used on an actual project or play)

Understanding plotting and story can be difficult because we are all brought up with stories, through being read to as children or watching TV and films.

But breaking the concept down into fragments can seem a difficult, perhaps even pointless, process. However, if a new playwright wants to avoid always telling literal and linear stories, learning how to break a story down is necessary, and to do this the difference between story and plot must be explored, creatively.

As I've discussed, story is the sequence of linear events that happen. Plot is how you as the writer organise these events and how you choose to tell the story. Because most people are aware of myths or fairy tales, I often ask student writers to do the following:

1. Think of a myth or a fairy tale you know really well.
2. On scraps of paper or post-it notes write each single event on a single piece of paper (for example, three bears live together in a house/three bears leave the house one morning waiting for their breakfast to cool/a girl called Goldilocks, walking through the woods, notices the house and walks in/etc etc).
3. Once you have each separate story event on a piece of paper, look through them and try to order them in a different linear sequence. So, for example, if you start with Goldilocks walking through woods, she is the protagonist and not the antagonist, but if you start with the bears then they may be the protagonists and Goldilocks the antagonist. What if the bears find Goldilocks in the bed at the start, and you lose all of the story prior to that? You might have to reveal what would be the backstory of why the bears left that morning and how Goldilocks came to be in the house. What if you start with Goldilocks in the bed, and it transpires that she turned up there the day before, has been sleeping the whole time, and the bears leave the house before breakfast because they want to discuss, out in the woods, out of her earshot, what they are going to do with this intruder?
4. Once you have a different order, rewrite the new plot you have created through the linear disruption, and then turn this into a short 10–15 minute play, set in one location. If you are in a group, you can ask a number of your peers to act this out for you, to see if your plotting stays true to or subverts the original sequential story.

Exercise 5: Location (sole work (but can be shared within a group) – creative exercise)

Because theatre cannot move to many locations very easily in a naturalistic style, as TV and film can, where you choose to set your play is crucial.

This exercise helps the writer explore ways in which location affects the characters and the plotting:

Write a scene, set anywhere, with two characters, one of whom wants something from the other character. Try to make this a concrete something for ease in the exercise rather than an emotion or concept. The scene needs to be around two A4 pages long.

(If you are in a group, once the scene is written you can ask two other participants to read this out for you so you can hear the dialogue.)

Now, take this scene and redraft it, but place it in one of these settings:

1. At the top of a mountain, in a hut or tent, during a storm
2. In a city centre bus station at 3 am
3. In the Ritz Hotel, in London, during afternoon tea

Consider this before redrafting: why are your two characters in this new setting? What changes for them in this new setting? How does this affect what it is that one of them wants from the other?

(If in a group, ask the same two participants to read the new draft out, and discuss how this changes the character dynamic and the theatricality of the piece.)

Consider why you would be asked to change the location of a play and what does this do to the piece of writing. Does it make it more interesting or more tense? Does it make the characters react in different ways, and how does it affect what character one wants from character two? Consider how you could implement this idea of location in a piece you are currently writing.

Exercise 6: Economy and exploration of language (sole work – creative exercises)

Several of the contributors had exercises which I would class under the heading 'exploration of the economy of language', and which I have grouped here as such:

> **Joe Ward Munrow:** Describe a journey to wherever you are, as simply as you like. Then rewrite it, but take out a consonant, for example F – so you can't use any words with the letter F in it, you have to find new words. Then rewrite it again but take out F and L. Then F, L and K – then take out all but one of the vowels – so you end up only being able to use, for example, words with the vowel I and the consonants B, G, H, M, P, S, T. It then breaks down, and it puts language under tension – but it means you can get to the core of character and story.

Billy Cowan: I ask my students to write a scene with two characters A & B. A is asking B out on a date. I then get them to do it again but with the restriction that each line of dialogue can only have six words or less. I then get them to do it again, with a maximum of three words per line of dialogue. This exercise shows them how the imposition of form can enhance the content and find new, more dynamic and expressive ways of communicating.

Fin Kennedy: (a) Limit the amount of words per line characters can speak, because when you first begin writing you massively overwrite. Even experienced writers in first drafts do it, so limit the words to say five, or even one; can you tell a story with no words, just actions? By which I mean characters doing something to or with each other, not waffling on. So, could you write this play entirely in stage directions? It should be possible to get a broad sense of the story by doing that. And then allow one word per line, see where that gets you. Audiences are smart, they will read between the lines, and they will keep up, you just need to learn to trust them. And actually, the old adage: Less is more – audiences quite enjoy having information withheld and having to try and work out what is going on. It gives them something to do and makes them actively engaged. So just as an exercise, an artificial limitation on how many words per line, or even if you allow words at all.

(b) I developed six word plays, which is just six lines of one word each, two characters, but you arrange them in such a way that they are in couplets, so there is a beginning, middle and end; there is actually a scenario that plays out, even in six words. There is no extraneous information, so you can ask questions like who are they, are they male or female, where are they, what are they talking about, how do they know each other, it is a stimulus to get over fear of the blank page, and it unlocks the imagination, and you write the play before you know it.

I also have a similar exercise to limit dialogue, because Kennedy is correct in saying all writers in first drafts overwrite the dialogue, over explain and add in far too much exposition or explanation of backstory. This is a Mark Ravenhill exercise I first came across when working for The Open University on their Advanced Creative Writing module, and which I have adapted and used for students since then:

1. Create a scene between two characters that is about half an A4 page long, with one character asking something of the other character – the restriction is that for the dialogue you can only use the word 'Yes' or

derivatives (yeah, aha, OK, yep). This means you really have to think about the world, the situation and the story you are telling. You can use as many stage directions as you wish.

2. Now, rewrite the scene, but you can add the word 'no' and choose one other single word, of your choice, which can be repeated.

If you are in a group you can ask two people to read out the redraft or even the original. This may seem like a bizarre exercise, but not only does it cut down on dialogue, it also forces you as the writer to think about circumstance, situation, character, location and what the objective is, and then write around this.

Exercise 7: Performing work (sole or group work – creative exercise or work on an actual play or project)

One of the concepts around writing for theatre that new writers have to get to grips with fairly quickly is that of the actual performance of the piece, of the work going into the hands of others to be presented to an audience. Performing your own work may be a hurdle to get over first.

> **Steven Luckie:** Write a poem. Which is an extraordinary way into writing, because you've got a voice, and then you have a platform, and then you've got to read your poem out loud, and that can start a piece of theatre.

Luckie's exercise of writing and performing something yourself, which is not necessarily a piece of theatre, gives the new playwright a way into the idea of performance.

> **Lizzie Nunnery:** I often read my work out loud as I write it, particularly if I'm writing monologue, to help me to feel the rhythm and flow and keep the spontaneity of the language. If there's an overworked phrase or overloaded sentence in there you know it when you read it out loud.

Reading your work out loud or having people read the work out loud for you is vital for the playwright because this is the medium in which the writing is meant to be communicated to an audience. So wherever possible, I ask students and writing groups to read each other's work out, so that the writer can hear it for themselves. If you are not working in a group, ask family or friends if they will come together to read your work out. Another option is to read the work out yourself, but record it and then listen back at a later date.

Exercise 8: Plotting (sole work – on an actual play or project)

You have started writing your play and you get a bit lost, a bit stuck. The work does not seem to be going in the direction you hoped for and you do not know how to get it back on track. Does this sound familiar? Well, all writers hit this point and there are a few ways to go forward.

> **Kevin Dyer:** Often writers get stuck because we think we don't know the answer but actually the problem is that we don't know the question – all those simple questions like: where is this scene? Who is in it? What is going on? All those 'w' questions – what does she want?
>
> What is different from the beginning of the scene to the end? Why is this scene here?
>
> Ask yourself those when you get stuck.
>
> **Chris Thorpe:** If you're stuck with a play, write the final line or the final thing the audience will see before it's time to clap and go home and work towards that.
>
> And it is not about achieving that moment, it is about giving yourself a flag on the horizon, and saying I have no idea how to get between here and there, but at least I know there is a 'there'. And the 'there' might change as you're doing it, you might end up in a completely different place, but at least you've got something to loop some rope around and try to pull yourself forwards.

I also find it useful to move away from words and to find a visual way of telling the story. This can be done in several ways:

1. Storyboarding – again most often linked to film making; in fact it was a film maker who introduced me to storyboarding. You do not have to be good at drawing, stick figures in pencil or crayon will do, and you can download and print off six or eight frame storyboards quite easily, and then imagine what you are seeing at each of the pivotal moments in the plot.
2. Imagine the story arc as an upside down tick:

By putting each of the incidents from the storyline along an actual line, I can see the physical arc of the story, and this works as another form of anchor to go back to if I get stuck during writing, which is an adaptation of Freytag's pyramid:

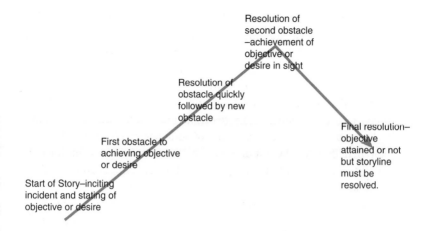

Resolution of
second obstacle
–achievement of
objective or
desire in sight

Resolution of
obstacle quickly
followed by new
obstacle

Final resolution–
objective
attained or not
but storyline
must be
resolved.

First obstacle to
achieving objective
or desire

Start of Story–inciting
incident and stating of
objective or desire

Theatre shapes

A final thought in this chapter is on theatre shapes. It may seem an unusual thing for the playwright to consider, but the audience experience can be affected by the space the production is played in. To prove the point, Zosia Wand and I both saw the same play in different venues. Wand saw it 'in-the-round' and I saw it on a proscenium arch traditional raised stage, and we both had very different reactions. For me, I felt distanced from the play and did not enjoy the experience very much, the action seeming to be directed in too insular a fashion, whereas Wand felt immersed in the world and had a good theatrical experience. Understanding how the formation of the acting space can affect your production for the audience is important to the writer, even though you may never get the option of choosing the best shape; this will come down to whoever commissions the play and who directs it. Whilst you may be more concerned with how your play appears on the page, how the physical form helps to tell the story for you, it can be useful to think about the sort of space you might write for. This is not about 'directing' the play whilst you write it, it is more about learning to visualise your work with the aim of 'seeing' how the audience may experience your story.

You may already be aware of the traditional proscenium arch raised stage type of theatre, with rows of raked seating for the audience in the stalls and the circle or balcony. But there are other types of staging, the most popular being:

- In-the-round – this is exactly what it sounds like; the action happens in the middle of a space surrounded by audience seats. This has the effect of involving the audience quite directly in the action and in the shared experience, because not only are you facing the actors but you are also facing other members of the audience. Examples of in-the-round theatres are The Octagon in Bolton, The Royal Exchange in Manchester and The Stephen Joseph Theatre in Scarborough.

- Thrust – this is similar to in-the-round, but the audience are only on three sides. This means that there can be more in the way of set on the back wall but there is still that sense of audience involvement. Thrust is a sort of halfway configuration between the traditional proscenium arch and in-the-round, and a good example is the main house of the Sheffield Crucible Theatre.
- Traverse – in this configuration, the audience is on two sides of the playing space, opposite each other, forming a type of corridor for the acting space. This is often quite popular in studio theatres.
- Promenade – this type of theatre has no fixed acting space but a series of acting spaces which the audiences walk between. It is very popular for site-specific pieces of theatre (where a piece of theatre does not happen in a theatre building at all but in a specific place, for example a warehouse or a car park) and for outdoor theatre events.
- End on – similar to a proscenium arch set up with the acting space and audience, often in straight rows, directly opposite each other, but the auditorium may be raked and instead of a raised stage the acting space is often at floor level, again a popular choice in smaller venues or studio theatres.
- Studio theatres – these often have flexible configurations and can be changed to suit a variety of acting spaces. They are often smaller in size.

It is useful to note that some directors or literary managers of buildings may really like your play, but cannot see it happening in their particular space, because, for example, it is a more intimate piece that needs to be set in-the-round and they only have a raised stage proscenium arch space. Whilst this can be frustrating for the writer, it does not mean that you cannot set up a working relationship with that theatre, as your next play may be better suited to their space. Remember, initial rejection is not necessarily the end of the road, but it does help when sending out your new play to show an awareness of the theatre and therefore the theatre shape you are sending the play to.

Conclusion to Part 1

In this first part of the book I have attempted to set a baseline for you to work from as you learn about becoming a playwright. Knowing your theatre history, being critically and culturally aware of the world around you and immersing yourself in the world of theatre, especially exciting new writing, all helps prepare the theatre-geek-in-waiting.

The building blocks and exercises should help you create a first draft of a new play, perhaps even your first play. Part 2, Speculations, will now help you explore creatively in new ways, as well as give you an idea of the theatre world you might be stepping into.

Part 2

Speculations

Introduction

In Part 1 I gave you the basis for writing your first play, the history, background and building blocks that are useful to know before you begin the first draft. The second part of this book assumes you have now written your first draft, and so it considers the place of theatre, and therefore the place of writing for theatre, in the current climate and speculates on the future of both, creatively and critically. Continuing on from Part 1, 'critical' means analysis of theatre in its various forms, engaging critically with the medium, rather than exploring a particular theoretical point of view, because even when creatively speculating it is important to remember that, as a writer, critical analysis is a useful tool alongside all the craft techniques you can learn.

I will explore new possibilities and ideas around creating theatre, through the contributions of those interviewed, continuing the collaboration theme from Part 1, but there will also be reference to some current publications and productions to assist in the exploration of where theatre could be heading in what we may call the digital age. However, I am wary of giving specific digital platform examples simply because technology is moving so fast, these examples may be out of date before the book even goes to print. So for the speculations about how theatre may interact with digital technologies I will talk in more general terms around the 'digital age'.

I am asking several questions in this section. For example, how relevant is theatre now? How can writers innovate, experiment and explore creatively? How can writers subvert traditional theatre writing – and has it in fact all been done before? Do audiences even want experimental theatre, or are we better off with good stories told well? Is there room for all these different types of creative work in modern theatre? However, I may not answer these questions, but continue to consider potential answers through consideration of the current culture and debates surrounding theatre, giving some pointers to where new writers can begin their engagement with the wider theatre world, allowing you to work speculatively on plays and write for performance in ways that may innovate.

Literary managers and dramaturgs will perhaps be more prominent in this part, as they work to develop new writers and are therefore constantly looking ahead, often a few years ahead, in terms of programming new work and finding new ways of working. But there will also be a consideration of existing work that may help playwrights navigate this ever changing world, as well as a brief section considering the work of the dramaturg and dramaturgy, and what these terms mean.

I may not be able to offer answers to all of the questions this section poses, but considering creative solutions and new possibilities is something theatre has always had to do. Because I am discussing the making of theatre, you will find that passions run high with some of the contributors here, but this is because theatre means so much to them. In a digital world, theatre can seem both archaic and still vital. Why, you might ask, should anyone go out to see live theatre when they can stay in the comfort of their own home watching a vast array of TV shows and films? On the other side, it is important to consider what the social impact of losing one of the few socially shared experiences society still has would be. As this issue is of primary importance to the future of playwriting, and a central argument when it comes to the debates around theatre, it is where I will start the next chapter: what does theatre mean in the twenty-first century?

7   Exploring Possibilities

The 'death knell' for theatre has often threatened to ring, and yet new theatre companies, new writing and new performances keep being brought to new audiences. Despite this being the age of the screen, the digital age of instant gratification through the Internet, as well as the Western world experiencing a range of austerity measures, with culture budgets continually being cut, theatre still manages to find a way to flourish and develop in new directions. This chapter will explore why theatre is still important to society, why we feel we still need theatre and how we keep theatre relevant. But first, it is useful to explore the types of theatre that currently exist and consider the help they can offer the emerging playwright.

Types of theatre

Theatre splits broadly into three areas, commercial, subsidised and fringe. I will look briefly at these three areas, although there is sometimes considerable overlap and whilst this list is not in any way definitive, it will give you a fair idea of where the money, support and opportunities are, and perhaps help you decide what type of theatre writer you want to be, or even how you can work with these theatres in new and speculative ways.

Commercial theatre

Commercial theatre does exactly what its name suggests. It is theatre that makes money. It is the long-running West End shows that open in several countries over a matter of years and have many changes of cast. These shows cost a lot of money to put on, so they need to earn a lot. Because they are considered commercial, subsidy is rarely available from arts councils or other public sources. But funding or financial support from private donors can happen, in which case there is all the more pressure to be commercially successful, so that those who put the money up in the first place can see some return. Commercial theatre is a business and it is often pure entertainment, such as the musicals, the comedies with TV stars in them and the celebrity pantos. This is an area where a writer may earn a lot of money, but also, without taking anything away from the entertainment aspect of these shows, there is rarely much in the way of creative or artistic experimentation or speculation in the commercial sector. That is not to say this never happens but it is very rare.

Commercial theatre often tours to large receiving houses in cities outside of London, a receiving house being a theatre that never produces its own shows but simply takes tours in. There are receiving houses in many towns and cities, and often they are old music halls ('Varieties') or opera houses. Runs may be a few weeks or a few months in theatres outside of London, whereas commercial shows in the West End can run for many years.

The shows are produced by large production companies which are not tied to any one theatre space, although of course some of these companies may own theatres as well. Currently there is an interesting trend of films and TV shows being recreated on stage through these big companies, which are a fair commercial bet because of course the audience knows exactly what it is coming to see. And all theatre comes down to being able to tell a story to an audience – a point worth bearing in mind, because there is a certain artistic snobbery surrounding commercial theatre, in perhaps the same way there can be artistic snobbery in the literary world about more commercial 'pot-boilers' being published. But I would make the same argument for populist or more commercial areas of creative production: commercial novels get people reading, whether it be detective thrillers, romances or kids' books about wizards. Perhaps if audiences go to see a few big commercial hits and enjoy themselves in that shared experience, they may keep theatre a living, breathing art form and be encouraged to push their own boundaries by going to see something in a rep theatre or even a fringe theatre.

So commercial theatre may be a good entry point into the concept of theatre for an audience member, or for a new playwright beginning to explore critically what can be done in theatre, but it may not be the best area to work in if you wish to be creatively and theatrically speculative.

Subsidised theatre

Arts Council England (ACE), according to its own website (www.artscouncil.org.uk), began life in 1940 as the Committee for Encouragement for Music and Arts, and began funding creative organisations after the Second World War. There are also the arts councils of Northern Ireland, Wales and Scotland (now Creative Scotland) who work on a similar model, supporting the arts through funding from public monies, such as the National Lottery. Theatre companies have always been major beneficiaries of funding and despite the ups and downs faced by arts councils, many theatre makers still benefit from their funding.

> **Fin Kennedy:** There has historically always been two strands of income into the ACE: one is grant in aid, which comes directly from Government and sustains all the National Portfolio Organisations (NPOs) for their annual grants – basically it is for bricks and mortar buildings (and what goes on inside those buildings of course) and some touring companies. Secondly, there is money from the lottery which funds discrete pots, like Grants for the Arts and other ring-fenced pots [which any artist can apply to].

Kennedy has done a lot of work on the current state of funding for British theatre, sparking discussion with politicians about the cuts in funding. Subsidised theatre is, arguably, where the majority of new theatre is created, and why you will often find that theatre can be such a political arena. When organisations are constantly having to fight for their right to exist through funding from Government and public monies, then it seems clear that they would become increasingly political.

NPOs include a range of smaller theatres and theatre companies that produce their own work in house (known as producing houses). Many of these theatres used to be known as 'repertory' theatres, because during much of the twentieth century they would run a series of plays, usually classics and well-known comedies, with the occasional new play included, across the year with the same company of actors and crew. Nowadays, producing theatres will run a season, usually from September to May of three to four week runs, although more and more theatres are now running summer seasons as well. It is usually the job of the artistic director, with the approval of a voluntary board of directors, to programme these plays. Lawrence Till has been the artistic director of The Octagon in Bolton and The Palace in Watford:

> **Lawrence Till:** There is a different responsibility between the nature of creating plays and curating plays, or curating seasons of plays at a venue, as an AD, because inevitably within that you have a responsibility for creating something new, but also making familiar pieces of work surprising as well, so there is a degree of reinvention every time.

The kind of planning they have to do ensures that they will have a few plays that will do well because they are known to be popular, either because of the writer, the story or the 'star', alongside a family show at Christmas and one potentially risk-taking new piece of work.

Many producing theatres run in a similar fashion to this, despite location or size, and it is worth developing a relationship with your nearest producing theatre, because it is most likely to be this building that houses writing groups, youth and community theatre groups and have a new writing associate or literary manager whose job it will be to support writers in a variety of ways, including having a resident or associate playwright or a writer on attachment. They may also run new writing competitions, playwriting competitions and offer opportunities if you get onto their writers' mailing lists. They may have two (or possibly more) theatre spaces, often referred to as the main house and the studio, which means that new writing can often get a chance in a smaller theatre space, the studio, without the venue having to incur the financial risk of putting on a brand new show by an unknown playwright in the main house for a four week run, which is usually how long a play in a rep theatre will run for.

Theatre companies who receive NPO funding are a little different, for whilst they may have office premises, they will not have their own theatre space. They will produce shows that tour, sometimes to subsidised regional theatres as well as smaller London venues, though probably not in the West End, on a smaller scale than commercial theatre tours. As a rough example, an NPO theatre company may tour to 400–600 seater theatres, whereas a commercial theatre tour may go to theatres that seat between 500 and 2,000. Fringe theatres (see more below) are usually 50–150 seaters. The touring companies who are producing new work, like producing theatres, may also support writers through opportunities, paying a resident or associate playwright or running a writing group. Publications like *Contacts*, which is published every year, or websites like The British Theatre Guide (http://www.britishtheatreguide.info) are a good place to start researching these companies and organisations.

To begin your relationship with a producing house, it is worth having a script that is polished to the best state possible to send to them, often referred to as a 'calling card' script. They are unlikely to produce this play but it will open up the conversation between you as a writer and the company as producers and this is the point where they may offer you some development, either for the calling card script or for a new idea you might take to them.

Development can come in a variety of forms:

- Dramaturgy – the literary manager, dramaturg or director may go through your script with you, asking you questions about your play in terms of characters, story, form and structure and what you are hoping to achieve in terms of audience experience for this work with the expectation that you will go on to re-draft.

- Workshopping – this can be from one day to one week of work with the script, a director and some actors, and can work in a variety of ways, from simple read-throughs and discussion to improvising around the scripts, acting out those scenes the play does not show or even complete re-writes.
- Scratch performances – these can be simple, as in a rehearsed reading, or can amount almost to a full performance, but it will be in front of an audience who will give feedback afterwards. The audience may be invite-only or paying (obviously aware of what they are coming to see) but they will be prepared in advance to give the writer and company feedback, which again will lead to redrafting.

There are also a few development agencies, like Playwrights Studio Scotland, who offer similar developmental services to playwrights. Sadly, many script development agencies, especially in England, lost their NPO status, and therefore their funding, a few years ago, forcing these organisations to close down, so this type of developmental work has now mostly fallen to subsidised producing theatres and companies.

Fringe theatre

As its name again suggests, fringe theatre is on the outer edges of the theatre world, but no less important for that. Venues are often smaller and may not be so well equipped, often above pubs or in small, out of the way buildings, and are run by people passionate about new theatre. This is where most theatre makers start out and where much theatrical experimentation, both good and bad, begins. You may already have heard of the Edinburgh Fringe Festival, which involves theatre and comedy, and if you live in London you may be aware of many fringe venues. If not, simply do an Internet search for London fringe theatres. But it may seem that there is not much else going on outside of these two cities and to a certain extent that may be true, although due to the ever changing nature of theatre and theatre funding, fringe theatre rises and falls in popularity in a cyclical fashion. At the time of writing, it is doing relatively well. Due to a number of factors, arts council funding, particularly from ACE, for individuals or small groups of artists is more accessible than ever before, which means that many cities currently have new fringe events, if not quite festivals yet, and new fringe venues. Of course, if you are really keen, any room above a café or pub can be turned into a theatre space – remember, all you need to create a piece of theatre is a room with some people sitting in it and some actors telling your story.

Whilst some theatre makers love the freedom that fringe theatre gives them, and will therefore always work in fringe despite the lack of money for both production budgets and income, for many it is the access point into subsidised theatre, to create a profile and experiment creatively with new work, and because of this fringe is vital to the theatre industry.

There are, of course, other areas of theatre, such as children's, community and youth theatre, all of which are useful for the writer to find out about and may become the main area of focus for a career in writing. Many of these types will usually be housed in a subsidised theatre or company, and there are lists of a range of theatre companies that are useful to know about at the back of this book.

Amateur dramatic groups can also be useful to the new writer, and they are usually quite accessible, being linked to many community centres, schools and voluntary organisations. They can be a good starting point for you if you find the world of professional theatre a little daunting to begin with. But the important thing to consider doing when you first think about sending work out is to find a theatre that is local to you, build up a relationship with it and so get their support as you move forward in your writing career.[1]

Theatre in the digital age

The digital age, as we may term these first few decades of the twenty-first century, has created changes in the way society views television, film, listens to music and engages with friends and family. It is therefore no surprise that some people have suggested that digital technology means that theatre will become perhaps more elitist. The argument suggests that because we can be told stories in new and satisfying ways through a variety of digital platforms, only people who already go to the theatre will continue to do so, and of course this number will dwindle as the audience ages. There may not be a new, younger audience to take their place. The risk then is that theatre moves away from being an important part of the British cultural landscape. But exactly where does theatre currently sit in our cultural landscape anyway? Should theatre entertain, expand knowledge, be accessible for all and be used as a public forum for debate? Or should it become even more elitist, be revenue based and be a spectacular once a year treat for the average member of society? And who is

---

[1] For example, think about Lizzie Nunnery talking about how important the Liverpool Everyman is to her, or Zosia Wand talking about The Dukes in Lancaster, in this book.

responsible for new writing? Is it, for example, theatres, development agencies or writers themselves?

As mentioned above, most producing houses are subsidised by arts council grants, which often seem to be consistently cut rather than increased, leading to these theatres having to attempt a more commercial view of the seasons they produce and often taking fewer risks as a result. On the other hand, many emerging playwrights are setting up their own ventures, such as theatre companies, mini-festivals and new writing nights, to gain experience in having their work performed, and also in the hope that a director, an agent, a producer or literary manager may come along to see their work. A few years ago, a theatre writing agent was considered a nice luxury, but not vital. However, more and more playwrights are perceiving agents as important to their career progression. Is this a sign of the commercialisation of theatre, a sign of the saturation of theatre writing in a dying industry, or simply a sophistication of the system, as has been seen in the case of novelists and the publishing industry? I have no answer to this question, but it is worth keeping in mind when speculating where theatre and the culture of theatre making may be heading.

An important question for the theatre maker to consider is: what is the point of theatre? Thinking back to its history, explored in Part 1, the purpose of theatre was originally to tell tales from the bible or myths of the gods, or to show the lives of the aristocracy and society's history, often to an illiterate audience. Now, however, we have high levels of literacy and more information via screens than we often know what to do with; we can watch game shows, reality TV shows, news channels and soaps on devices whilst travelling on public transport or in the comfort of our own home. So why do we need to leave the house, pay out for travel and parking, a meal perhaps, babysitters and quite expensive tickets, often to see something that we may or may not like, something that may or may not entertain us? These are the questions I have put to the interviewees and this chapter will explore some of their answers.

What we cannot get away from currently is the funding crisis that has hit theatre alongside the recent austerity measures. However, as mentioned above, funding crises have always hit theatre, and it is interesting to look at the differing reactions to the question I posed to interviewees about the current theatre climate.

> **Steven Luckie:** You've heard of social engineering? This is social elimination. I think there is a cynical, genuine attempt to change the model of public funded theatre to the American model of philanthropy. And it won't have much of an effect in the short term, but in the long term

we won't be the world leaders in theatre. It will go, we will lose our place, we will vanish.

Short term, to save money, the changes that are being made will have a profound effect. We take it for granted that people from other countries want to come and see our theatre. That a large proportion of the UK celebrate in every single town the effect theatre has on television, film and music, in every area you can imagine. We lead because we have some of the best actors, we have the best directors in the world, I don't even want to go on about it. But why do we have to put everything down to pound, shillings and pence? It works, it works brilliantly. That tiny investment? You get ten-fold back. We are not America, we don't have the American constitution, and we have to accept that. [...]

It is disastrous, I think it is absolutely terrible. I just don't believe in philanthropy. It can take a place with certain rich people, but there is also the other side of it – if a person is investing in theatre, then what are they investing in for? Is it for themselves or is it for the people? The beautiful thing about subsidised theatre is that it is for the people. And we have it in abundance, so philanthropy is already failing. Just talk to all the theatres, they are going to start shrinking. We have now reached a very dangerous point, and don't measure British success by what is on in the West End, there is some excellent stuff but much of it is rubbish or very commercialised. Can we take that sort of risk? No we can't.

Twelve Angry Men finished here at Birmingham Rep last Saturday and is going into the West End, and you could say the reason the West End is booming is because of subsidised theatre with its mix of work. But you know, theatre is not finished yet. Playwrights should perhaps pray...

Other theatre makers, whilst recognising that we are at a difficult time for funding in the arts, suggest that perhaps this might be a better situation for emerging writers to be in, because there is less reliance on the producing houses Luckie speaks of as core to theatre production.

Rob Drummer: I am perhaps going to be really controversial and say we are at a really exciting moment. I'm sure a lot of people will say we are in a bad way, money is tight and isn't it awful that there is less and less enthusiasm for the arts. I want to flip that. I could go and do talks and say that it is really bad as a new writing theatre we are still surviving on the same size grant here as when we were over the road above a pub, give us more money, and I could consume my week with simply doing that. Or I could just say, well wouldn't it be nice to have more money and more time, but let's work with what we have, and find the best work to produce. I think we make a much stronger case for the arts by fighting to produce exceptional work, exceptional art and open that up to as many different people. And this is not me being naïve, I would love to commission three times as many writers as we do, of course I would. Because I can't, I don't want to bemoan that, I just want to make sure that the right writers are being commissioned. [...] At a time of limited resources, the instinct is to programme safely, to take less risk but the reality here at the Bush is to take more risk. Taking those risks opens up a huge network of organisations who want to support us, and I think it is the ambition of the artist that secures that support, whether it be time or actual money. [...] Playwrights must understand those gaps, understand those narratives that are not being staged, and to write that work. [...] Playwrights forget that they have a choice. They think sometimes it is an isolating career and that you are sat alone in your room for ages and then ultimately you are at the mercy of anybody who reads your play. Turn that around and what you have is that everything starts with the writer. Don't think: I'm sat here waiting for my plays to be produced; think: I am sat here waiting to write those plays that can only be produced, now. It is the responsibility of the writer, agents, directors, to say here is the question I am asking, I am being specific, here is the experience I have. [...] It is about connecting micro questions to much larger issues. That connection to your work, to be able to spiel about it because you live it and you know it, and having the headspace to think about the work that is important. So I think it comes back to social responsibility, if you want to see your work on stage, understand the fight and the conditions theatres are working under as well as the work we are trying to make.

The big play you want to stage may not get commissioned, but that does not mean there are no other ways to get your work out in front of an audience. This is a huge debate in theatre because, as Luckie points out, much commercially viable work begins in the, admittedly larger, regional theatres that are subsidised by the arts council through their National Portfolio. This work takes time and money to develop and it is a concern for all those working in theatre when the chance to make work like this is threatened by funding cuts. However, the flipside of the argument is that the arts council are still funding individual artists and groups of artists to create work, and it is this coming together that Drummer is speaking of. The idea of moving forwards to a new form of creating theatre that does not rely on the building based theatres is becoming more of a reality. Of course, the danger here is that the divide between big theatres and more experimental fringe work will grow ever wider.

Lizzie Nunnery: Another impact of the cuts to the arts is more anxiety in literary departments and artistic teams about filling seats and selling tickets. I can definitely see that more people I know are getting commissions to work on projects that are adaptations or have a big actor on board, or both. Or maybe it's a new play but they've got the actor or a local story they can sell. I think you can really see the marketing now, and I can understand where that comes from – it's out of necessity. But at the same time it's really important that writers continue to write the stories that they're desperately driven to write. There is absolutely a place for a new adaptation of *Jane Eyre*, and I would probably go and see it, but there also has to be a place for that new play: that story and those characters that just did not exist before. Writers have to write from themselves, from their own strange places and their own strange voices, and it could be that we see more of a separation between the big venues and the fringe venues. I'm not pessimistic. I think the weird individual new plays will keep being written and produced, but we'll see less of them in the big established venues and fewer risks being taken in those venues over the next 10 years. However, I'm hopeful that there will always be big brave companies who manage to make the budgets work and have the creative bravery to still put on those plays in the big established spaces.

Fin Kennedy: Our working model confounds capitalists because it doesn't really work as a moneymaking plan, but does that make it valueless? Well no, not really. We have to try to reclaim the debate of how we measure value, not just in the arts but in education and the wider society really. I mean, it is nothing new, it has been going on since Thatcher, this wholesale marketisation of every aspect of our lives, and the only measure of value is cash, and that is just unintelligent. There are so many types of value in the world, but we seem to be beholden to this single measure, this market Methodism, what Phillip Pullman called free market fundamentalism. And it is a form of fundamentalism. Whenever you say there is only one of anything, one power, one thing we have to answer to, you become a zealot. Unfortunately we've got zealotry that has crept into the mainstream systems. I wouldn't like to be starting a career now, you need to get a day job really.

I do have faith in the public, that the public understand there is more to life than that. I believe we are broadly liberal and humane as a nation, actually, but those are very powerful arguments backed up by very powerful vested interests. That is part of theatre's job too, to describe and illustrate the channels of power that operate in any situation, not with any overt political aim, but just so we are an educated populace that can sit outside of itself and the day to day, and actually be citizens in that sense of who are we and what do we care about collectively. And what sort of a world do we want to live in? There are fewer spaces to do that, but theatre is one of them.

Kennedy, along with other theatre makers, believes the industry is 'terrified of the new' and yet it is the responsibility of playwrights to keep producing the work because, as Kennedy points out, there are still people who want to experience live theatre, even if the industry is struggling to find a working model that fits with a capitalist society.

But is theatre still important to our society?

Writing for theatre is in its essence about writing a form of entertainment. This is a statement that may well be queried in many European theatre companies where the art form takes a more political social position, but in Britain there is the bottom line that the theatre company is asking the audience to pay to be entertained. It may be creative work that happens, it may ask wider questions about the society we live in, but it is there to give the audience a specific experience that they cannot get elsewhere, which is key to theatre's survival in the digital age. So who, then, is responsible for ensuring that new work is being produced and taken out to that audience?

Kevin Dyer: Where do you start on this one?

The people who programme theatres have got a difficult one because some things will sell and some things won't, and often if it is an unknown writer with an unknown play, then it is hard to sell.

I sometimes think as writers we have to write great stuff that is irresistible, because you know *Billy Elliot* was at one time a new play, *Blood Brothers* was a new play written for a small young people's theatre company in Merseyside, now probably one of the biggest plays in the world. So we must not lose space for new plays either as writers or as theatre producers.

Shakespeare's plays were all new once. Even though he used stories that were used before. Shakespeare probably wrote the plays which were irresistible for his time because he wrote about his world. The dangers for us as writers is that sometimes we try and think with producer's heads on – what would the audience like? Oh, I'd better go and write a play about

Angelina Jolie or I'd better write a play about celebrity or I'd better write a play that's a spin-off of Strictly Come Dancing, and this is not the way for writers to go.

I am willing to bet also that there are more new plays put on in the UK now than there were 20 years ago. The only problem is that most writers don't get paid for their first new plays. I think that is a really troubling thing in British Theatre. More and more theatre practitioners are working for nothing – writers, actors, stage managers. There is an increasing profit share culture, particularly with the use of people who come to get training in theatre. Theatre companies are propped up by volunteers. What is frustrating for me sometimes is you'll go into a theatre and the people working behind the bar are being paid, and the people doing security are being paid, and the accountants are being paid, but actually the actors and the writer aren't, and I think this is becoming increasingly common.

But oddly enough, I think the arts council are hugely supportive of new writing, I think they are easy to knock. And I think lots of companies are supporting new companies and new writing, there are lots of seed commissions and little umbrella schemes, but there does come a point when companies have to put their money where their mouth is and support new writing properly and fully.

Dyer suggests that there is a responsibility on writers to ensure the work they are doing is good, the best it can be, and that those who create exciting new work will always somehow be produced. This does call back a little to the traits of being a playwright I looked at in Part 1, where tenacity, drive and ambition were all considered an important part of being a playwright. Even if work is rejected, the message from these theatre makers is: keep going.

Lizzie Nunnery: Playwrights have a responsibility to keep working at their craft, and to speak up for their plays and be bold in finding ways to get them produced. Theatres have a responsibility to find a way to put great new plays on their stages, which actually might mean taking the risk of not attracting a huge audience. Marketing departments and Outreach departments within theatre companies bear some responsibility to find new and perhaps unconventional ways to get people to plays or plays to people.

The arts council have a major responsibility and it's important that we don't let them shy away from it. If we accept the cuts they've put in place for new writing in theatre, and instead look to corporate models or kindly benefactors to fund our work, then we're in danger of being complicit in their withdrawal of support. More than anything it's essential that new theatre stays in the hands of the artists and therefore a culture of theatre supported by charity or private investors worries me deeply.

And there is a need for new stories to be told all the time in a world that is ever-changing. The argument that there are only so many stories, so many plots, holds weight for writers, and it is sometimes useful to think about the piece you are working on in terms of archetypal character or in terms of plot points or beats. But audience experience, considering what most affects an audience and therefore what most affects you as the playwright, must also be considered. Writing that particular story at this particular time in this particular place. In telling somebody's story, whether it is based on a real person or whether the character is entirely fictional but still tells the audience something about the world we live in, the audience connects and empathises with the 'person' they are listening to on that stage.

Holly Race Roughan: Artistic directors need to nurture new writers. It is absolutely fundamental that new plays are produced. A tiny militant part of me feels like there should only ever be new plays because the one thing theatre can do is respond to its environment immediately, and I feel that if theatre is a place where we learn to understand each other and the world we live in, then what better way of doing that than by putting on new plays by people who live in the world that we live in now.

If theatre is going to be a happening exciting place that says something about the world we live in, we should only be programming new writing – occasionally put on the great classics to remember where we came from – but what are we doing if we are not putting on new writing? Doing old plays in new ways is great but it is never going to be as cutting edge as doing a new play. I believe it is better to have a story you haven't heard before, rather than an old story you've heard before, even if it is done in a new way. You wouldn't be impressed if the Arctic Monkeys released the same album twice with a twist, but you do want to hear their next new album of new songs, and I think that it is interesting that the music industry makes its money from new songs whereas the theatre makes its money mostly from old plays. Is that a mentality shift, is it because we're so obsessed with Shakespeare? Why do we not have the same thing with music or film? It would really excite me if the norm was new plays and every now and then we banged on a Shakespeare. But then again, good new plays are hard to find, but that is just an argument to put more time, energy and money into the development of new plays!

Zosia Wand: New writing has to be subsidised in some form, otherwise it would be impossible to sell new work without making the tickets too expensive, it would become too exclusive. You just have to look at commercial theatre, how expensive tickets in the West End are, for example. And also the quality, it has to be guaranteed, obviously popular, no risk involved, no experimentation. We should be striving for new work.

[So responsibility lies with] Writers (to produce the work), artistic directors (to recognise potential of that work and support writers in producing the work), the arts council (to fund all of that process in some form or other, to support and fund the writing, the development and the production).

With most people involved in theatre making, there is often an egalitarian view that theatre should be for everyone, that it needs to be, as Wand states, sensibly priced to encourage audiences to take a risk on new work and that as an industry of theatre makers we want to avoid making theatre so expensive it prices out all but the most wealthy. There are currently various schemes that involve subsidised price tickets for young people or students, which often work well, but the fact remains that many of the producing houses are still having to charge between £10 and £15 for a ticket, despite government subsidy through the arts councils, and often this funding is cut year on year.

Elizabeth Newman: In the age of austerity I still believe that if you write good work it will be produced. The issue is that artists are getting a bit distracted by the financial climate, and they're not concentrating on why an audience aren't going out as much. And it is not just money. If you ask people, have you cut down on your drinking? The answer will probably be no. But they won't be going to theatre, because theatre is not part of people's 'life diet' in a way it might have been 400 or 500 years ago. Why isn't a ten quid ticket to the Octagon Theatre in Bolton worth sacrificing two bottles of wine? I kick it back to the artists to spend some time thinking about that; I know I spend a lot of time thinking about this.

Newman's point is a consideration for all those working in and loving theatre, but I do worry that there is a sense that writers have to respond to this by writing plays that will be 'safe' to ensure 'bums on seats'.

There are many debates about where we are to find exciting new theatre, beyond the safe slightly commercial programming. Where are we to find exciting new playwrights and what we are doing about the clashes in the debate between art and creativity and box office receipts? As a playwright, all you can really do is keep creating the work and to try not to have a producer's head on when doing so; however, being aware of these debates around the culture of theatre making is a vital part of working in the theatre world.

> **Suzanne Bell:** If you look at someone like Enda Walsh – when he started out, him and his mates in a back room in a pub in Cork put on play after play after play, that they would quite often write really quickly. And they'd be quite short, and people would come, and there was no money, but he learned very quickly what worked and what didn't work, and how to manipulate his audience. So when it came to writing *Disco Pigs*, which arguably kind of launched him, he knew exactly what he was doing, he knew exactly what buttons to push, because he had gone through that experience of going, oh right, that didn't work, that was a bit rubbish, that was problematic, that didn't hit the note I thought it would hit, I wonder why? It's not just going: look I've put my play on; it is about going: I'll watch the audience as they experience my work so that I know when it's not working. The writer is always responsible for their work. If you look at reviews for Shakespeare or the classics it is the director who gets the reviews because it is the director's vision; for new work, it is the writer because the writer is at the heart of it.

The writer is at the heart of all new plays, and a brief survey of the current climate would suggest that there are a lot of opportunities for new writers out there, often clustered around London, but regional opportunities can also be found. These opportunities can take the form of master classes, writers' groups, writing projects, competitions or pitches. They are useful for the development of your process and of your writing, and should be seen as an opportunity to learn, network, make new connections and get your name 'out there'. If you can go on to set up something new with your contacts, putting on plays in the back room of a pub with your mates, then so much the better.

In this section, much has been said about the arts councils and how funding cuts are affecting British subsidised theatre, and this can be quite a confusing area for new writers. Fin Kennedy, who created the In

Battalions Delphi Study of theatre funding, explained above the situation regarding the funding of British theatres through the arts councils, which bears some further exploration here to fully understand the current debates:

Fin Kennedy: The implications for the sector and for how we make work and how we get new writing out there are quite interesting, because you've got the bricks and mortar side reducing, and so theatre companies in the historical and traditional sense of buildings and bricks and mortar and touring are kind of dying away, particularly outside London. There has also been a recent rule change with the arts council whereby companies can't apply for Grants for the Arts for top up funding or for specific projects, but the side effect of that is that there is more available for individual artists, which means the balance of power is shifting, and we are seeing more individual artists applying for their own money to do projects, in small scale collectives or even individually, and we're seeing a generation of artist/producers and even artist/performer/producers or writer/director/actor/project managers emerging, and that is great. Obviously the political backdrop is worrying but in terms of who is responsible for ensuring new writing gets to audiences, the channels by which they get there are changing. If this trend continues then I've heard it said we might be looking at a sort of return to a 1970s Joint Stock model of the artists doing it on their own. We've built up a huge infrastructure over the years, obviously those buildings aren't going to go anywhere, but they are very expensive to run, and the economic business model of theatres is not particularly profit-making, not through any fault of its own, it is just that the costs are quite loaded and audiences are necessarily limited physically in capacity, so that may not be an economically sustainable model without subsistence of some kind, but it might be that the exciting new work gets done on a much smaller scale, more emerging artists getting together in a co-operative and going out on the back of a truck, whilst we get a risk of branded fodder in the buildings, because of the funding situation.

In some of my In Battalions Delphi Study stuff there was a question about lobbying the arts council to change the rule allowing NPOs to apply for Grants for the Arts and this did not score highly, partly through artists protecting their dedicated funding pot, but also several comments saying if theatres who are in receipt of regular funding are not prepared to spend that funding on risk-taking and developing new work then they have no right to call themselves theatre companies, they should not have to apply to a top-up pot for new writing. New writing should be the life-blood of what they do and of theatre, and I kind of agree with that. We are not America, we are somewhere between America and Europe, but we have a model that should allow some risk taking and should allow some slack in the system to not make the obvious choices and to try and involve the art form with some creative risks, so I do think there is a responsibility from those building based companies to ensure new writing gets to audiences.

But I also think audiences have a responsibility, you know, use it or lose it – if you value new plays, go and see some new plays more than once a year if you can, that is ultimately what counts to the arts council, is how many people will come to see this, how many people is this attracting, and it won't be the greatest show of your life every time you go, but every now and then it will be. And I still think that is worth doing.

Perhaps to ensure theatre still appeals to younger demographics, to keep theatre relevant to society still, young writers need to ensure that work is produced that invites rather than alienates new audiences.

Lawrence Till: Theatre is one of few, rare communal celebratory events where people get together to hear stories told, you go to the cinema, there are only four or five people there, you go to church for weddings and funerals and christenings and Easter and Christmas – regular church-goers are essentially going to hear stories, but theatre is one of the few places where you can celebrate and have things affirmed, that you can learn things about yourself and about the world, and that you can be moved, excited, inspired, laugh, cry, and you don't get that sat in front of a YouTube clip – you can howl and share it with a few mates, but not 600 people or so. And the degree of commitment you make when you get a ticket and sit down, sit for an hour, have a break, sit for another hour, that is a different sort of commitment that you make watching the telly, watching the telly, you can record it, you can pause it, whereas a play will happen at 7.30 pm and if you're there, great, you've seen it, and if you're late, you missed it. So you commit to it differently, and that makes it unique and a bit more special.

The nature of theatrical participation now is probably no different from other interactive things that were happening in the 1960s. You had site specific and interactive theatre then. There are cycles of theatre, people want a well made play, they want an interactive piece of storytelling, if you look at the digitisation of theatre that happened in the 1990s and people were putting films in, and that stopped because we just got bored of it, and it doesn't really happen so much anymore. The technology has become much more efficient, but I think the experience is still important. People want to go to theatre for an experience. I've been to secret cinema, where people think they are in a film, which is even odder, and I didn't particularly enjoy it, it wasn't to my taste, but thousands of people taking part in this interactive event, and we all sit and watch a film, it is the same as a circus, it is about what is the added dimension that we can be given? It is best value, what do we feel are we getting extra?

Writers need to engage with the wider world and take something new to the audience. Playwrights can no longer exist in a vacuum in their bedroom or study, writing plays that perhaps tell of their relationship with online gaming. Playwrights have to exist in the collaborative world of theatre. They have to understand what work is being commissioned, what work is not being commissioned, what types of plays work in which types of theatres, and then make conscious decisions to work with or against that world to create theatre that they are passionate about and that says something about their world. As Till says above, theatre has always moved in circles or cycles, trends come and go, and each new piece of technology is taken on board and refashioned. Theatre exists simply because those who write and create theatre want to share something in a room with other people.

> **Elizabeth Newman:** I think giving people access to how theatre is made through digital means, like time lapses where you can see a set arriving, a writer tracking the development or sharing research, to give the audience an insight, is really interesting. Where I get spiky is where digital is used to replace other live forms of expression, like an actual set. [Physical Theatre Company] DV8 are phenomenal about including digital stuff and integrating it fully into their live performance, lots of other companies stick up a flat screen and show what we can see on stage, which I don't understand.

> Theatre is a social experience – digital stops the shared experience, because it is a relationship between you and a screen. When it is you being a voyeur with other voyeurs, it feels different. There is something like DV8's *Just For Show* (which explored the insular relationship between media and sexuality, where they had a spinning projected globe around the world that I remember being amazing) or your piece of work [*Project XXX* by Kim Wiltshire and Paul Hine] where you have young people interacting with the screen, which are both different to just whacking up a flat screen and projecting a castle on it because we're in a castle: some people would consider that digital media – I don't.

But also, let's be clear, theatre is not enjoyed by all. The industry should make great art for everyone, that should be the objective, but I don't like going and watching sprinting, I don't want to be made to watch sport because I don't enjoy it. Let's not believe that we are creating a marvel, that if people don't enjoy it, they're somehow not getting it, or we're not doing it new age enough for them. It might just be that they prefer going to the football.

Whilst theatre must not exclude, it should be remembered, as Newman suggests, that some people simply do not like theatre, in the same way some people simply do not like horror movies or fantasy fiction, or football, or snooker, or live music gigs. Playwrights can make work that speaks to particular audiences using new digital technologies, and even bring new audiences into the theatre building with this, but it must fit with the audience experience you are trying to create.

Fin Kennedy: I think if you look at the work of companies like 1929 and that sort of animation/live crossover, I'm not sure that would have been possible in the same way 10 years ago. I had an idea about doing a teenage play using something similar, I sort of wanted holograms but they don't exist yet, but I wanted to do a play about a kid who draws a lot and whose characters come to life in the play. I'm sure that sort of stuff will become a possibility, and I quite look forward to that. The arts council does a lot to encourage digital stuff and have these funding pots, which is great and fine but there is a bit of frustration for me in that there is this idea that digital is an art form, and it is not, it is a platform; actually the content, the most important part, is still pretty analogue, and that's about ideas, and people and artistry. So, I'm not too obsessed with the digital and I don't think theatre is either. I think we should integrate with it in the right way and not just because we can, and that will take time to work out.

The technology enabling streaming of live performance and archive work is also of current interest, with sites like digitaltheatre.com and NT Live bringing people together and providing an opportunity for those who, for example, live in more remote areas to see large companies do big plays. The flip side of that links to the comments I made earlier about commercial theatre, and the same argument works here: does seeing an NT Live performance encourage more live theatre going or less? If an audience member enjoys a live streamed version of, for example, The National's *Frankenstein*, might that encourage them to go to a new play put on above their local pub? And what can playwrights do to address this variety of media vying for the audience's attention (and money)?

> **Rob Drummer:** Playwrights must understand those gaps, understand those narratives that are not being staged, and then go and write that work. If writers come in with a fully formed proposal or an early draft that speaks to our contemporary reality, to our contemporary culture and a commitment to a question that is not being asked and that can only be asked of this audience now, then that writer will get ahead. If you can inspire me sat around a table every week meeting countless writers and through your play provoke with a question that we as a theatre should be asking our audience, then I will fight for that work to be developed. Playwrights have to engage with the realities of what it means to put on a play and also what it costs the audience members to come and see the play. Writers also need to understand about timelines, playwrights genuinely think that they submit a play through an unsolicited process and that six months later it will be on stage.

There is practical and creative advice there, and this perhaps gets to the heart of the debate, of what kind of playwright you think you might want to be and then working out who you can go to, who you can work with, to help you achieve that work.

> **Kevin Dyer:** To succeed in this current climate, find people who are like-minded to you, actors and directors, film makers, puppeteers, and make theatre with them. Because theatre is a collaborative act. You can't do it on your own, you really can't. The other one for me is to remember that Arthur Miller is dead, so there is a lot of space for us to be great writers. We don't have to fall in behind anyone else, you just have to have great ideas and make them fantastically – that's how you do it. Make yourself, your ideas, irresistible.

The concept of collaboration and finding people you can work with keeps coming up and is something I will explore more in this section, but it is important to remember that there is no magical solution – no book on writing for theatre can give you that. The bottom line is: only you can write what you can write. And it may be that the script that comes out of that story becomes your calling card script, becomes the one that introduces you to a number of theatres but is never produced, but remember that those introductions lead on to a developing relationship and hopefully 'greater things'.

Holly Race Roughan: A writer should write the play they want to write, not the play you think someone wants to read. Go and see as much theatre as possible – a playwright friend of mine reads a play a day when he can. There is a kind of chemical make up to plays, and we need to work out what that make up is and know what the building blocks are in order to be able to challenge them. But knowing how a 'typical' play works is important. I am a massive believer of learning by doing, just writing and writing, get friends to read it out loud for you, and getting stuff on at the fringe or at university, you will learn so much from doing that.

The overriding message from all the theatre makers I spoke to is that as a new writer you may have to find other work and lower your expectations, but that perseverance will produce results, for there will always be a theatre industry to write for, even if it does not conform to the type of theatre you originally thought you might be writing for.

Billy Cowan: For a playwright to succeed they need to diversify – do other work such as community, outreach work, mentoring, teaching etc. They also need to be able to network and develop relationships with other theatre makers and writers. They also need to be brave enough to put on their own work if they can't get anyone to produce it. Put it on and get it out there wherever you can.

A creative career as any type of writer is never going to be an easy one. There are very few jobs as a writer, where you can go into an office every day and produce work for someone else. You will probably have to become self-employed and you will definitely have to be very self-motivated. But even if you see these as drawbacks in the current theatre climate, there are still exciting possibilities:

Lizzie Nunnery: Because of the change in funding there is a shift that's happening – away from a wide culture of writers' groups and writers' courses for new and young writers. I think we're starting to see less of that and it's hard to predict the impact. I think on one hand there's the danger that the training isn't there – that there will be a lack of really skilled confident playwrights in 5 to 10 years. I can't speak strongly enough about the positive impact the Young Writers Programme at the Liverpool Everyman and Playhouse had on me. But on the other hand there's a little bit of excitement in me about the sort of writers you get with less training and more practical experience, and the way new approaches might be able to break through.

Regardless of climate, a playwright has to write and they have to do so not out of a desire to succeed in their career but out of a desire to create. They have to do it because they can't *not* do it. I don't believe anything else will carry you through the strangeness or the isolation of being a writer in a room on your own battling with a play, not once, but over and over again.

All the theatre makers I interviewed made this same final point: you have to do it because you cannot NOT do it.

Hannah Tyrrell-Pinder: Roy Williams says – don't get it right, get it written. All playwrights should have that above their desks.

8   Cultures of Writing for Theatre – Innovators

In Part 1 I considered some great theatre innovators of the past, but when I asked interviewees who they thought of as innovators, quite a few of the names that came up were of people working in the now, with some of these being near the start of their careers. This means that some of the people discussed below may be unknown to you, which is a good thing since it gives you an opportunity to find out about work that is happening now, in this century, and work that is most relevant to you and the world you live in. And if someone mentioned here piques your interest, then please go and research their work, or even better go out and see it, and find out about their critical and theatrical beliefs. These innovators are relevant to you as a new playwright since you will be following quite closely in their footsteps and you should be able to find their work more easily, if not live then at least online.

> **Kevin Dyer:** I think we are at a really exciting time in British theatre, I think lots of people are making lots of different plays in lots of different ways, and that is really exciting. It's not just about a bloke sitting at home, writing out of his head and sending it off in an envelope or sending a document via email – it doesn't work like that anymore.
>
> The other night I saw Matthew Bourne's *Swan Lake*, and it left me breathless, and this isn't a piece of theatre, it's a piece of dance which is still a piece of theatre, it's an event, it is about Britain, it is about young men, it is about relationships, it is about a lot of stuff, but it felt very alive. It was fantastically constructed and performed. So this week it is Matthew Bourne, next week it will be someone else.
>
> I saw a piece by Travelling Light a few weeks ago called *Boing* which was a piece for young children, but it uses B-Boy, so it is about dance, but it is about two boys the night before Christmas, and that was exciting in its form. Hardly any words, is for kids, but beautifully structured and a lot of fun.

Innovation is about the new, and sometimes these experiments work and sometimes they do not, but as a writer or theatre maker it is important to understand the idea behind the attempt at innovation. Considering some of the ways theatre can be innovative when accessing current theatre culture, exploring what is happening in theatre other than musicals or star-named shows in the West End, is a useful creative tool for any playwright or theatre maker. Every time you visit the theatre or read a play, consider the techniques that have been used: Have you seen this before? Is there reference to what has gone before or has the writer ripped up the rulebook and done something that is completely different to anything you have seen before? And how can you, as a writer, incorporate innovations, build on them and take your theatre piece in a whole new direction?

Innovation for the playwright is not just about the words, or the dialogue, or the storytelling. As Dyer mentions above, dance and movement can be just as important as a form of theatre that we all experience. But what do they do for an audience? How can they enhance experience?

Holly Race Roughan: Hofesh Schecter, who is an Israeli born choreographer. Most recently I saw *Political Mother* at Sadler's Wells and it is just epic storytelling. They had three different levels on a very deep stage, and they took out all the stalls, so they had this sort of mosh pit for the audience, which gave it a sense of occasion which you don't normally get in theatre. The room went to blackout and the middle level lit up, they had fourteen violinists and cellists, who played the opening, then the bottom level lit up which was filled with drums and a rock band, then finally the ground level, and the collaboration between the dance, choreography and the lighting design was just immense. It depicted all these images with no real narrative but it was looking at the individual versus the system, and it was so exciting and so engaging and you felt you were at a concert, rather than in a theatre. For me, theatre has got to embrace or relearn a ritualistic sense of occasion and special occasion rather than falling back on polite theatre going.

Ella Carmen Greenhill: I would suggest something really recent that I saw in Edinburgh by With Wings Company. I can be a bit funny about physical theatre, when people say 'physical theatre' I kind of switch off, but this was the absolute meaning of physical theatre: there was this guy in a washing machine who fought his way out of it, and about ten minutes in I thought I was going to start crying, not because it was a sad play, but because it was just so brilliant and so different to anything I've seen and that made me feel really emotional. I thought, the fact that they've made me change the way I feel about this, that I'm not sat there going 'oh this is rubbish' (and I'm sure a lot of physical theatre is amazing, and I'm not saying I know loads about it) but I just felt that every single movement and every single awkward thing that they were doing wasn't just to say: look, I can do this because I'm very fit – it was to create an emotion in the audience and it was just beautiful.

There is of course the argument that each new piece of theatre will have some form of innovation attached simply because it is a new piece of theatre, but I am talking about more than that here. Looking back to the past to see what has gone before experimentally is useful and gives new writers a solid foundation to work from, but looking to the present to see what is happening in theatre now, and what might excite you in theatre terms, gives a sense of the cultural landscape you might go on to work in. And it is a very wide cultural landscape that you are going to be joining. Now, it might seem that there is too much to take on board here all at once, and it is not my intention to alarm or confuse you at all. So – go slowly. Research different types of work, use your pen to highlight names or cross names out; research work that is relevant to you, and keep a journal of your thoughts about theatre scripts, performances, craft texts and theories. This is an ongoing process and, as I said earlier, all writers are continuously learning. It is no different for you. Now you have the basis from Part 1 to build upon, you can speculate about new ways of creating work, but this will still take thinking time, pre-writing time, research and consideration of which theatrical direction you want to go in.

> **Suzanne Bell:** It kind of depends what area of innovation you are looking at really. You could look at the way in which technical innovation influences our experience, for example look at the work of Slung Low or 1927 or Illuminus. Or look at the way movement is used, so Hofesh Schecter's company – there are so many different innovators. [...] There's the classic sort of Robert Lepage, Peter Brook, Robert Wilson, Yoshi Oida, Katie Mitchell – I was a big Katie Mitchell geek when I was younger, and I sort of obsessed about her quite a lot. But also Sebastian Nubling, Thomas Ostermeier, Forced Entertainment, the Wooster group, Steppenwolf, Team – the list is endless.

Bell mentions here directors, writers and those who might be termed theatre artists from around the world and this global outlook is useful to the new playwright, for whilst, in terms of career advice, it is good to get to know your local theatre, exploring what is happening creatively and culturally around the world is vital. The digital age that I talked about in Chapter 7 has also led to a more global outlook on the cultural landscape, and a creative exploration of what is happening in Japan, the USA, Australia, Europe and

Canada is therefore easier than ever before and should form part of your
creative diet.

> **Ruth Little:** I don't have a single number one ranking for that title,
> and I think it would be a mistake to create a pinnacle in a realm which
> is based so fundamentally on relationship, collaboration, influence,
> dialogue – horizontal ways of working. I could rattle through the twen-
> tieth century greats whose work has had a significant cultural impact in
> Britain – Peter Brook, Brecht, Littlewood and so on, or hammer home
> the obvious in relation to Shakespeare. But that's for critics, commenta-
> tors and academics to do. On a personal level, my own journey has been
> affected at different times and in different ways by different practitioners –
> they might include Simon McBurney for his animation of image and
> idea, Peter Brook for his steady paring away of theatre/life practice to
> bare essentials of self-maintenance, Joan Littlewood for sticking it to the
> status quo, Shakespeare for anything you like, but they'd also include
> choreographers from whom I've learned more about language as gesture
> and the relationship between movement and meaning than I learned
> from the study of theatre itself – that would include Akram Khan, first
> and foremost, for his insatiable curiosity and magpie tendencies in com-
> bination with rare and astonishing craftsmanship, and Siobhan Davies,
> for her concentration on and attention to the overlooked and everyday –
> the reanimation of the neglected world. It includes Liz Lerman for her
> work with non-dancers and older dancers, because I think art without an
> ethic of broad and deep concern for humanity and human interactions
> with the world is fraudulent. And it would include Cornelia Parker, whose
> exploding shed is for me a complete expression of what a play can actu-
> ally do in the mind – take the familiar paraphernalia of life and atomise
> and reorder it into something new.

The idea of the past and present coming together to form a whole is also
clear in Little's list, and similar 'historic' names come up alongside those
creating now, such as Shakespeare, Brecht, Littlewood and Brook. But Little
also looks to other art forms as well, other creative artists who innovated
in their own field but whose creative ideas can feed into your creation of
performance pieces, and this breadth of cultural experience is something
all artists should aspire to.

But I am exploring the work of playwrights in this book, which means
concentrating on how an emerging writer can be speculative, can explore
new ways of working and be inspired by those theatre makers who are inno-
vating right now. It is interesting to note that the historical innovators in
Part 1 were mostly playwrights, but the contemporary innovators

mentioned by the interviewees in this chapter cover a range of roles. This may be because the making of theatre is becoming ever more collaborative. It could be that in the future, if not now, the terms used to distinguish roles disappear and we all become theatre makers as Radosavljevic (2013) suggests. Or it could simply be that in theatre we tend to revere playwrights when they are published and dead! However, some of the interviewees did mention current working playwrights as innovators.

> **Joe Ward Munrow:** The stuff that Chris Thorpe is doing is really important at the moment. In terms of me as a writer, it was when I read Crimp's *Attempts On Her Life* and I realised that it is just language, to me that just seemed like poetry on stage. Obviously there are other people you read later, like Sarah Kane and people doing different things with language, but for me it probably was Martin Crimp. Then something like *Getting Attention*, which was interesting because it is about the working classes, but is quite a straight play for Crimp, but at the same time he's still doing the same thing, like the language is used so well, you realise that just because you are using language in such a precise way, doesn't mean you have to be avant garde, you can use it and it can be a brilliant straight, working class, slice of life play.

> **Adam Quayle:** Simon Stephens – a huge hero of mine. I'm drawn to the way he writes dialogue, he creates a situation that on the surface is everyday but he has this stylistic quality to the dialogue that is really heightened. My experience with Simon Stephens started at the Royal Exchange when I was an usher, *On the Shore of the Wide World* in the main house, and I've tried to see as much as possible with his plays. I find the way he uses language to be innovative. I did English at Hull University, and so my background is very text based, which is why I like new writing.

But remember what Elizabeth Newman also said earlier: 'I would ban new playwrights from reading Simon Stephens because if I read one more rip-off play I might shoot myself'!

This is where a critical understanding of the way you are inspired by these innovators or the way you use that influence is crucial. Influence is not about copying or parodying, it is about critically examining what a writer or theatre maker is doing in their creative process. It is about understanding the techniques used, the structure, the language use on the page and how this then transforms on the stage.

That we are all influenced by the culture around us is clear, whether that be TV, games, movies or music. What you have to do as a writer is analyse why you are influenced by this particular piece of work, or artist, or writer.

Think about how it makes you feel, the elements or blocks that create that effect, then reassemble your own version for a new audience of the story only you can tell; in other words, apply this knowledge to your work. As I mentioned in Part 1, I remember when I first began to write scripts I was far too influenced by Pinter and threw pauses in all over the place, with non-sequiturs and uncomfortable comedic moments galore. And to be honest, that may well still be an aspect of my writing, the difference being that with experience comes acknowledgement. I know now if I am getting too 'Pintery' with a piece – I can recognise it and move on. When you decide to become a writer, a playwright, you have to take your place in the industry as it stands and become aware of what is happening around you, appreciate this work, enjoy this work, then forget it completely and create your own story in your own style. This might seem paradoxical, but through practice and development it will become second nature.

Bringing theatre to a new audience

As I explored in Chapter 7, the digital age and the rapid rise and change in technology does give pause for theatre makers to consider how to keep theatre relevant and bring in new audiences.

> **Rob Drummer:** I think it is important not to look at any moment past and instead to think who is innovating now and who will continue to innovate in the future. That singular artist for me at the moment is Sabrina Mahfouz, who is a performance poet, a playwright, a novelist, storyteller, producer and director; she is working across a range of art forms. She is absolutely committed not just to her own work but in supporting other spoken word artists and performance poets; she curates. She is one of the most exciting and driven young theatre makers that I know, asking contemporary questions of culture – and not just about theatre, which is really important.

> I find myself so much more interested thinking about culture rather than theatres talking to other theatres or critics talking to other critics. I think as an industry we enjoy that conversation with ourselves a bit too much. What I am seeing with young artists is a real appetite and drive to speak to contemporary culture much more broadly, and as a result of that, putting theatre firmly within a broader culture rather than putting it in its own culture. And Sabrina epitomises that. She has been generously supported through Ideas Tap, she has been an associate artist here at the Bush, she has a night of spoken word performance poetry with POP, which is happening at The

Southbank Centre and coming to us as part of Radar, the festival here in November. But she is also writing these wonderfully ambitious pieces of theatre, the first one of those being a show called *Dry Ice* which she also performed in and was at Edinburgh a couple of years ago. And with each piece of work asks questions of form, story, culture much more broadly, gender, sexuality; she is on this really fascinating journey in that she will pull in all sorts of references, will refashion those, will re-appropriate those. There is an attitude in her work that really connects to an audience, there is an international element to her perspective, she is looking further than the end of her nose. And she is someone that lots of people are going to be unaware of, but I believe in the space of the next couple of years, the form of her theatre will not only benefit from all of this stimuli but I think for audiences there will be a clear sense that this is theatre of a generation, for a generation and defining a generation. And in that respect she is innovative.

Chris Thorpe: There's certain pivotal things – I went to see Forced Entertainment do a show called *Speak Bitterness*, it would have been in the mid to late 90s, and that was a process led show in that they set themselves a task and just did it on stage. The task was just reading random bits of paper on which was material that they had carefully chosen according to the task they had set themselves in the rehearsal room and, again, you see the influence of that kind of theatre. They weren't the first people to do that, although they may have been one of the first British companies to do that so explicitly, and they do these huge grand scale shows which are fantastic, but that particular show, which was seven of them I think, was quite small, quiet and simple, was just brilliant. Whether that's an innovation or not, I don't know because I didn't know enough about theatre at the time, but it was certainly pivotal for me in that it said: this is also theatre and this is a shared human experience and makes a virtue of showing its mechanics. They're a company I've gone back to again and again, but any show that has that quality of just slightly re-jigging your understanding of what that contract is in that room is really beautiful.

And I've got that from working on student shows as well, it's not just about the big established companies. There's a show that came out of Dartington College called *When You Cry In Space Your Tears Go Everywhere* which I come back to reference as one of the most pivotal shows I've ever seen. It was very much influenced by art and performance art of the last few decades, in terms of tropes and it had people reading things, sometimes deliberately badly, and it had a kind of irony to it, and if you'd seen it done not by a bunch of people who were 19 years old it might have felt like a bit of a cliché. But when you watch this type of work done by people enthused by the possibilities of the stage, and not just thinking that any material they create is good enough, because they're doing it deadpan, but are actually interrogating and producing quality material, it was re-energising for me and fantastic. And equally to see an interesting and well made play, say something by Chloe Moss, to see the work she did with Clean Break, and *This Wide Night* particularly, in terms of seeing conventional people on the stage asking you to believe that this room is something more than this room you're just in.

The work I've done with Third Angel and Unlimited, that falls somewhere between the play and the live experience of people just having a conversation, all these things are massively influential. And I'm aware there is a canon, and I'm aware of that canon with all its various strands of performance and poetry, but those beautiful pin pricks of light and inspiration are not from the biggest companies that you see. They're from moments when someone manages to pitch something perfectly to be a great example of what it is. And it doesn't matter if it's a play or a crazy live art thing, where it is 49 people in a swimming pool full of jam. For me it's about theatre that excites and replicates the music I really like – the poetry I like. Emily Dickenson plainly didn't give a fuck about anything other than getting her poetry right, and that is incredibly inspiring. Bands like Minor Threat or Fugazi, that I've seen live, that have completely redefined my idea of what a gig can be, not necessarily through artiness but through sheer energy and excitement – these things all feed into my hope of what theatre can do, that don't necessarily have to be the big canonical things.

Energy is a key point here, brought out by both Thorpe and Drummer. New audiences, which usually means young audiences, need to recognise that there is something in theatre for them, that something is being created for them, and looking beyond the strictures of theatre can be useful for this. Harnessing the energy that is created when you go to a gig, and attempting to bring that into a piece of theatre is a very exciting creative challenge. How do you do that? Using different forms of live performance and collaborating with other artists and art forms is something that I will go on to explore in the next two chapters of this part, but it is worth pausing to think about those exciting moments that happen live but not just in theatre, and how as a writer you can learn from that.

Who can new playwrights learn from?

Building on the exploration of the debate and current culture of theatre in the previous chapter, I want to consider those innovators who may be more behind the scenes, who are currently creating or assisting in the creation of theatre, and who emerging writers can therefore learn from. This could include many of the people interviewed for this book, some of whom were, in fact, referred to by other interviewees.

> **Rob Drummer:** Playwrights now should also be learning from filmmakers and musicians, all those exciting YouTube channels that have started up as a place for original drama, that becomes an important place to learn from.

> Look beyond theatre as much as possible. I would much rather go to a gig, or a gallery or see a film or sit in a pub and talk to my parents or my friends, I would much rather do that sometimes than sit in a theatre five nights a week.

> **Ruth Little:** Learn from visionary and always-searching choreographers such as Akram Khan, Siobhan Davies, Sidi Larbi Cherkaoui, they might learn about language as a form of gesture, about the rituals of exchange and relationship, and about the meaning of stillness.

> From natural scientists they can learn about chaos and complexity; the forms that dynamic matter takes at every level of scale, and about systems theory more generally.

> From ethicists and essayists such as Rebecca Solnit, they could learn that art can be part of the mutable world, rather than 'a monument on its banks'; they might be encouraged to look for the connections between things, recognise that their own interventions in these systems have value and meaning.

It comes back to wanting that breadth of knowledge and that hunger for the new that were some of the important traits needed by the playwright explored earlier. And Suzanne Bell makes a similar point about going out of your comfort zone as a playwright, about continually learning.

> **Suzanne Bell:** Go out there and be a sponge. I remember sneaking into sociology lectures when I was off work, I learnt so much from that. There is this idea for playwrights of don't go and learn about playwriting, learn everything else. Learn about life, learn about the way people interact, the way other people view the world, learn about post-structuralist language structure, learn about surgery – and not just because you're writing a story about someone going into surgery, think about it in terms of how

it might influence your work or the way you tell stories. You know Chekhov, Ibsen were not just playwrights, they had other professions, that gave them a view of the world, a view of life, life experiences that weren't just about theatre, but it's the lens through which they then see that and go, how does that influence my work as a writer?

Bell is talking about more than simply entering a few terms into a search engine and seeing what the Internet brings up here. She works with hundreds of writers, at various stages of their careers, but treats each writer as if their work is the most important piece she is reading or working on at that moment, and if a literary manager or dramaturg is affording your work that much respect, you as the writer should approach your writing with the same attitude. The literary department of your local theatre is incredibly useful, a point which Elizabeth Newman makes, because it may offer you the opportunity to join writing schemes or writing groups, which can help the new writers to workshop and discuss their work. (There is some practical information for playwrights about this in Chapter 11.)

Widening your own cultural knowledge, contacting literary departments of theatres and becoming aware of the industry in terms of working playwrights and theatre makers around you, are all vital tools when looking towards innovation in the theatre of the future. For many of the innovators mentioned in this chapter that is the path they followed; they are aware of the world around them and want to pose questions to the society they live in about the society they live in. Much of the advice from the theatre makers I interviewed has been very positive in this chapter, but I will end with a final word of warning from Rob Drummer, dramaturg at The Bush:

> **Rob Drummer:** There is an attitude and an energy coming out of every new writing theatre that isn't accidental or random, it is the culmination of conversations around the writers we are ambitious to produce. And by and large we are reading plays about alien babies and spaceship set plays that have no question at their heart, plays that have no shape, plays that feel flabby, plays that feel as if they were written overnight and then just submitted. Playwrights need to engage in what is going on around them, not in a careerist sense, but putting on stuff in opposition to other writers I think is a really exciting place to be, whether you are starting out or already established, understanding where you are on that continuum can only be beneficial. You should write the plays you want to write, but you should understand where those gaps are, where is the gap that you can fill, where does the experience only you can have fit? That comes from a close working knowledge of theatre history right up to the current moment and then embracing it or rejecting it and refashioning it for your own purposes.

9 Exploring Practice: Making Theatre in the Twenty-First Century

Currently, there is a fairly traditional way of writing for theatre, with a clear process consisting of three stages:

1. The playwright writes the play, either as a calling card script to send out or for commission.
2. A dramaturg and/or director agrees to develop and/or produce the play.
3. The play is presented to an audience in some form, whether as a read through, a scratch performance or full production, in collaboration with other theatre artists.

There is nothing wrong with this basic way of making theatre and since it has happened this way for many hundreds of years, why should we change it now? But in this digital age are we able to find new ways of making theatre?

Changing practice

As I have already discussed, subsidised theatres do a lot of the work developing and producing new writing. Being subsidised means, however, that these theatres are always at risk of having their funding changed, or cut or having new criteria applied. Subsidised theatre was considered vital to creative exploration in the 1960s and 1970s, but the sociopolitical culture then changed as a result of the capitalist economic model of Thatcherism, and the idea that the arts should be paid for in part by the tax payer was scrutinised much more closely. As Fin Kennedy has explained, arts council funding has always had the two main strands, but now there are an increasing number of artists, either individuals or small groups, capable of obtaining arts funding directly for themselves for new work – provided they have some sort of track record – without going through the traditional channels of sending their work to the artistic director or literary manager, who acted as 'gatekeepers' in the past. This does not mean those gatekeepers should be dismissed, far from it. These institutions will always be a vital part of getting theatre to new audiences. However, it does mean, as mentioned in the previous chapter, that emerging playwrights need to think about the theatre world they want to work in, and the relevance of their chosen medium to audiences now. Instead of being reactive to the changes in funding, emerging theatre makers need to be proactive in the ways they create new and exciting theatre. The first decade or so of the twenty-first century has seen a rise in the number of new theatre companies, an interest in different ways of presenting theatre and possibly more new writing than ever before.

The new technology and media also allow for some change in creative practice. They allow for experimentation and give diverse groups of people opportunities to creatively collaborate, even if, for example, they are not in the same country. But using new technology also takes into account the changing world around us, and it is this engagement with the wider world that interests many literary managers, directors and dramaturgs. It is not simply a case of saying the technology is there, I want to use it, but of asking how can I say something meaningful about my world, and what tools can I use to say it?

> **Rob Drummer:** I read a lot of plays on the page that feel quite nice, quite polite, quite small. You know they have thought: if I am going to get a play on at The Bush or the Royal Court it has to be like this or like this. They look at what they are experiencing in theatre, and write a very tight, and well written play. So the playwright who is being careerist thinks they are doing all the right things by getting their play on in a studio theatre or maybe an Edinburgh presentation that transfers to Soho – all these steps that playwrights have become a bit obsessed with. But actually for the season here next year, we are producing artists who are daring to ask questions, who, at the start of their career, are pushing at the boundaries, and we're saying, we are going to run that work for six weeks and we are going to take a real creative lead in making that work as brilliant as it can be. [...] We are struggling against people who can sit in front of YouTube and watch these amazing kind of short form dramas that are emerging, production companies like Kudos working with Dennis Kelly on *Utopia*, we are surrounded by really interesting storytelling that we can sit at home and engage with, or sit on the tube and watch on iPlayer. So if we fall behind on engaging with those new artists who are using those same platforms and same methods, if we are not putting that work on here, then how are we going to see an audience grow and change?

This interest in how to use digital platforms is something I will explore more in the next chapter, but the idea of new and emerging writers coming together to work across a variety of platforms, to not simply think 'I am a playwright therefore I must sit alone in my room and create a well made play and be commissioned' is one of speculative interest. The idea of bringing a variety of different types of work onto the stage, using content that attracts those people who do sit in front of their computer screens all day long, and finding new forms within which to tell the story simply builds on the tradition of collaborative theatre making that the playwright has always been part of. And finding new ways of making theatre together is crucial to the future of theatre, to keeping theatre relevant. If you think back to the innovators of the past explored in Part 1, and contextualise them, you will see that theatre for them was growing stale, becoming less relevant, and their innovation breathed new life into the medium. Theatre, as already suggested, does work in a cyclical manner and it could also be suggested that it is reaching a point now where theatre has to find new innovators to keep its place in the world. Like any form of culture, innovative practice settles into accepted practice, which settles into old-fashioned practice waiting for innovative practice to come around again. Within all of this, practitioners and theatre makers have to go back to the same question: how can I continue to make theatre relevant?

Some theatre makers feel they no longer have the right to simply make art because the question of who needs theatre and why, the question of what theatre is for, seems to be at the heart of all funding bids and all theatre programming, rather than who makes good art and why. The question of whether theatre appeals widely, democratically, or to a very small elite is always there, indeed many building-based directors and dramaturgs will talk about 'our audience', or ask of a new play 'who is the audience?', because they have to know the demographics of the majority of the people who will be buying tickets, because they have to make an income. And so the pure art for art's sake approach has to be dispensed with, because whilst new writing may be within a theatre's remit, so is getting bums on seats. Innovation can seem a distant dream and the question of what sort of writer you want to be comes about. And this is not a question of whether you are a 'good' or a 'bad' writer – many 'good' writers write brilliant Christmas family shows and many 'bad' writers get caught up in the, often incorrect, idea that they are artists creating work that speaks to the Brechts and the Littlewoods that went before them, even if they cannot get an audience for it because it does not provide a satisfying experience.

> **Zosia Wand:** To survive as a writer in this climate you've got to be able to make your living doing something else, as well as developing relationships with directors and theatres.

To earn money and survive as a playwright you need to have two heads on at once: head one must engage with what theatres need to put on to attract an audience whilst head two is writing what you want to write in your own voice and getting that work out there as well. It is a balancing act that is made more difficult by what is often deemed to be fewer new writing commissions coming out of theatres, juxtaposed against the wide range of development schemes and opportunities those same theatres are offering.

But this does not answer the question of why we still need theatre, of what it is for, how it is still relevant, when we can get all our storytelling at home through a variety of media platforms?

> **Rob Drummer:** We are losing the opportunities to come together collectively. Community is evolving, the sense of the communities we belong to are in a state of flux. If we look at those institutions that were really about people coming together historically: the church, theatre, a pub, village halls and summer fetes; those things that were about community, about being physically connected to other people. Over time, despite a brief resurgence in those British traditions we see on television, actual collective experience is dangerously declining. In its place I think we are seduced by online communities, digital spaces and hyper connectivity through the Internet. So theatre for me is an opportunity for the coming together physically of people, and as many different types of people as possible, sharing that story, sharing that communion. We benefit massively from having to be ourselves in the real world, from having to articulate ourselves in front of other people. Theatre means a lot, but it is about having a shared space. And our mission here (at The Bush) is that the shared space is open and plural, is for a community that exists, that predates us being in this building, and for a new audience. That plurality is important, and the physicality of coming together means something. Forcing yourself to have to talk to a person face to face. I read this fascinating article about how businesses are increasingly seeing amongst younger members of staff a reluctance to meet physically, and even on the phone to articulate themselves, there is this reliance on the written word, on email culture. And that is sort of terrifying; people are growing up further and further removed from human contact in real communities.

> For theatre to fight for itself it is important to remember that in the course of any evening of performance or event, the audience member is sat in a room full of strangers, sharing an experience which they may be singularly responding to. But what you cannot get away from is being one of many. This is why there is a resurgence of immersive theatre in many new companies, because that immersive experience takes this to an absolute extreme, in that being part of a shared experience means more to us.

Those things that we find funny together, those things that shock us, when you have that emotional response in a room full of people there is absolute value. For me it means a lot, but it comes down to that collective coming together of as diverse a group of people as possible and sharing that experience.

New forms of theatre

In Part 1 I explored some of the more traditional forms of theatrical story-telling, concentrating on Aristotle's Unities and the way that theatre pushed at boundaries and innovated in the past. I discussed how form and story are inextricably linked in theatre, so whilst the playwright has to think of the story they want to tell, and the question within that they want to pose to an audience, the next consideration will be the form and structure of the piece. If you think of Ibsen and contextualise his work in his time, or writers who used comedy and the musical to highlight social issues, for example Joan Littlewood or Joe Orton, it is clear that the telling of stories in new ways is something playwrights have always had to think carefully about, to ensure the best possible audience experience. Considering new ways to surprise, delight and excite a theatre audience, make them laugh and make them cry, but also make them feel as if the piece of theatre they are watching is leading them to ask questions of themselves and of the world they live in, is all part of the playwright's process. Remember that the new piece you are writing has to draw that audience member out of their house, away from their television, their box set or tablet screen. They have to choose to come and see your play.

A question that arose from this thought was: which productions entice theatre makers out of their house? So this is the question I asked the interviewees, because if you, as a theatre maker, expect people to come and see your work, it is worth considering what you would leave your warm, cosy home for on a windy, cold November night.

> **Billy Cowan:** *White Trash* by Quarantine at Contact in Manchester. Quarantine is one of my favourite theatre companies – creating plays with 'real' people using their own stories and lives. *White Trash* used a group of white lads from a council estate in Salford, I think. It was electrifying and poetical.

I also remember seeing this production and the exciting thing about it was that it challenged all the typical play conventions. There was a lot of 'telling' in terms of the narrative sense, rather than the usual 'showing', blurring of lines between reality and fiction by using 'real-life' stories through a mixture of dialogue, poetry and movement. And it was riveting – I had to stand for the performance, which was around 80 minutes straight through, but it went so quickly because the performance invited the audience into the stories that were being told.

Lizzie Nunnery: I saw *Crime and Punishment* at the Liverpool Playhouse, a co-production between the Playhouse and Glasgow Citizens Theatre. I thought it was astonishing: one of the best productions I've ever seen. What really thrilled me was the way Chris Hannan's adaptation worked with the staging – they had so clearly been conceived as one. There was a real awareness of storytelling and theatricality with all the performers on the stage all the time. Apparently the director went to Russia and observed Russian rehearsals and was really inspired by the style of the Russian rehearsal room. The stage looked at first like a random collection of shabby and beautiful objects. Then it was filled with these characters that were also in a way beautiful shabby objects. Then, in a Brechtian way, characters came forward to perform their scenes. I was really interested in the way that this meta-theatricality didn't in any way diminish the emotional involvement or belief in the story. I think audiences can be really sophisticated and handle that kind of double think: on one hand admiring the craftsmanship of these people putting this show together, and on the other hand absolutely accepting the reality of these characters and the stories that unravel. That was really liberating to see because as a writer I can become quite anxious about those choices and whether if you go down a route that's too aware of itself, you might alienate people from what you're asking them to feel or think. I really admired the way this enormous novel had been distilled, so that you didn't feel as if you missed anything, because the human heart of it was there – the big issues that beat all the way through the novel were present in the scenes the writer chose to put on stage. And it was very funny as well: the play managed to be both heartbreaking and hilarious, and the style of acting was so much about the moment. It felt like the actors were discovering the characters as they played them, not playing the backstory or everything that was going to happen to them afterwards. That might be a strange thing to say but what I mean is the performances were all about the energy in the moment, and the characters' particular relationship to each other scene by scene. I'm really interested in that idea of character and identity, and how sometimes in British theatre we pin down ideas of identity too much by over-emphasising backstory and defining a character's psychology and motivation before we even begin. Actually the way we live isn't that. We discover ourselves constantly, and maybe there's a rehearsal process that allows actors to embrace characters in that way a bit more.

Ella Carmen Greenhill also mentioned this very performance, saying how 'experiences like that remind you why you do this'. And that is a crucial point. Building up the kind of critical awareness that Nunnery alludes to above, that you can then bring to your own work to find new ways to use theatricality. So, in the *Crime and Punishment* example, this is a Russian novel adapted for stage and so the director visited Russian theatre companies for inspiration, researching how they work and respond to their own creative questions. Now, you might not have the opportunity (or the budget!) to do something like this, but there are other ways to broaden your creative horizons without spending vast amounts of money.

> **Kevin Dyer:** I loved the first half of *Billy Elliot*, it was fantastic. Matthew Bourne's *Swan Lake*. I was at the Take-Off Festival in Durham the other week and there was this Italian company, I'd never seen them before, and they did this piece called *Pop-Up*, where they just used pop-up books to make a piece of theatre that no British theatre company could make. Then, when I was in Iran, I saw a dance production of *Othello*, but of course in Iran men and women cannot touch each other on stage, it is illegal, and it was probably the most sensual, sexual piece of theatre I've seen in my life, as they tried to break all the barriers. When I was younger, I was about 16, I read *The Importance of Being Earnest* and just reading the playscript made me laugh and laugh and laugh, and I still remember kneeling on the floor of my bedroom reading Oscar Wilde and laughing.

> **Steven Luckie:** *Missing* by Gecko. What's On Stage said of it: 'an astounding mixture of dance, puppetry, and incredible stagecraft. One key element of *Missing* is that it holds back as much as it gives, granting only glimpses of narrative, lighting tiny sections of the stage at a time, and allowing only fragments of conversation half-heard, all of which leaves the audience disturbed and enchanted'.

> It deliberately has a tiny narrative and you have to think, you really have to work. One of the hardest and yet one of the most exhilarating experiences I've had in a long time. And what it does is it allowed me to go back to academia, because you can have the experimental side of you knocked out of you by working in regional theatre. That allowed me to go back to the experimental stage.

Sometimes, of course, we can be surprised at what influences or excites us. Chris Thorpe, whose work is both written and performative, and often devised, recalls how he was inspired by a piece that was not in a usual area of interest for him.

Chris Thorpe: I've seen some great stuff over the past couple of years. I've seen Chris Goode's *Monkey Bars* at the Traverse Theatre, seeing shows at the National and International student festivals, there have been quite a few stand out shows – but I'll tell you what the most exciting one was: a director I've been working with from the States, Rachel Chavkin, was directing a musical, well it was more an opera, called *Natasha Pierre and the Great Comet of 1812* by Dave Molloy and it is on Broadway, and I got to see the final run of that in the rehearsal room. That was exciting, and I'm not into musicals or opera really, I think they're prone to existing for reasons other than their need to be good art, but what I'd done was I'd convinced myself that's all there was about them, that they weren't worth my time in terms of going to see one. But to experience something that was in a genre that I had kind of given up, that had all the integrity and the energy and the cheekiness and the sheer emotional slap in the face that I saw in that rehearsal room, to experience it pivotally at the moment before it went out in the world, so energised with this beautiful score and this amazing story that it tells – it's just a single brief strand of *War and Peace* that it's based on – and to be there with a bunch of people who were just incredible at doing that, that was exciting. And again it really changed my attitude in terms of why we do this and that it is never a matter of genre and matter of underlying attitude.

And then the other recently is just the experiences I have had with Hannah Walker and making our work that is conversations with our audiences, which is how I make theatre. We get together and we make work that is specifically about a common aspect of being human, be it our mobile phone or our propensity for fucking up, and seeing the way audiences have engaged with that, particularly working through Forest Fringe who I think are incredibly exciting, they are a collective of artists that I'm involved in who include artists such as Lucy Ellinson, Andy Field, Abigail Conway, Tim Crouch, who have all done work there. Tim Crouch's play *The Author* I think was one of the most fascinating theatrical statements of the last 20 years. Seeing that was a pretty incredible moment.

Joe Ward Munrow: *The Author* by Tim Crouch I thought was amazing, and with what he's doing – well I'm not sure as a writer I understand what he's doing with semiotics and the symbolism within theatre and what things mean, and the way he uses his own name, and he plays himself, but it is not himself, and the things he says he's done he hasn't really, which is a really weird thing to do, and it blew me away. And his use of space, with the audience facing each other, and that feeling of communality, it was so disturbing but amazing, and brilliant – it made you do things in your mind, but it didn't force you to do anything, it led you to a really weird place and it made you think about theatre without being pretentious. That was really exciting, and when we left the theatre we talked about it for a couple of hours afterward, and we were really wound up, that we knew we'd had an experience, but I was still trying to work it out two hours later. Seeing good theatre companies is like seeing good stand-up, speaking as someone who does stand-up, in that you don't want to copy what they do but when they do something outlandish or amazing they inspire you to be brave in your own way. So, *The Author* for example is amazing and brilliant, but I wouldn't want to copy that style because it wouldn't be my style, but when you see someone be brave and take risks you think, OK, I can take risks as well, so I think it is more the inspirational as opposed to what they are doing on a technical level or with language or something like that. But that's the nice thing about theatre, isn't it? If you see something and it is brilliant, you think, I want to do that. If you see something that you hate, you think, I can do better. Whatever you see, you're still learning.

Finding new ways of working with form can be through using music, puppets, music acts or spoken word artists, visual art, immersive or site-specific work, and it can also be through multimedia or digital work. You might want to explore a more post-modern form for your theatre, blurring reality and fiction, perhaps even performing the work yourself. Ella Carmen Greenhill gives an example of a project she wrote for with a company who wanted to create the live experience digitally to show some possibilities for working in new ways:

> **Ella Carmen Greenhill:** The liveness of theatre is the thing – like the Skype thing that I did, I worked with a New York company, so I was the writer in Liverpool, the director was in Romania and the actor in Mexico. I met with Miguel on Skype and asked him about his life and Mexico, and he could tell me the truth or lie, and from that I created a short script. Anna, the director in Romania, and Miguel then worked together on the script. It was performed in an Internet café; one audience member at a time logged on and Miguel did his performance.

> As a writer I had to think about the liveness and interactive nature of it, so it was a bit like a computer game as it responded to the viewer's answers to the questions. I had to think about those answers because it was about making a real offer to the audience. Some theatre pretends to make an offer to the audience but hates it when it responds. I kept thinking about that for this piece, so each audience member had to have a real response: the person who answers 'yes' to a question needs to have a different experience to the person who answers 'no' or who doesn't answer at all.

So that was a really interesting experience because although this was digital, it still worked on the live principle of theatre.

Using new digital platforms is a way of allowing theatre to evolve and Greenhill's example highlights the importance for playwrights to see themselves as integral to the collaborative process as well as the writer's responsibility to think beyond traditional settings and traditionally theatrical ways of telling stories, whilst holding onto the core reason of creating pieces of theatre, and why creating this live experience still matters.

Ethnographic, verbatim and participant led theatre

Ethnographic theatre is, in its simplest terms, theatre that uses actual voices and real stories to create a play, either through research by the writer or through the involvement of the participants in the actual piece, and this is something that many of the interviewees have spoken about or alluded to. This real-life aspect can often give an edge to a piece of work, knowing that it recounts real people's stories. Considering previous advice theatre makers have given here on challenging and exploring the world you live in, and writing stories that only you can tell, there can often be a slight concern with ethnographic or verbatim theatre that as a writer you are co-opting the voice of another rather than using your own voice. However, it might be that a particular real-life story speaks very loudly to you and that in fact you are giving a voice to a story that the world needs to know.

Verbatim theatre is often linked with ethnographic theatre. In verbatim theatre participants of a community are interviewed and then their actual words are used in the script. Alecky Blythe has done some interesting work in this area, concerning big issues such as 9/11 and 7/7 as well as the London riots of 2012. It is worth looking at her work and considering the audience experience, or trying to see one of her productions to experience it yourself. There are some issues with this type of work, again often to do with accusations of inauthenticity, as Duska Radosavljevic explores in her book *Theatre Making: interplay between text and performance in the twenty-first century* (2013), where she suggests that:

> By acknowledging that the very process of transposition of reality onto the stage will throw up its own limitations and potential accusations on the groups of 'manipulation of facts', it is possibly more honest to once again seek to stay faithful to the language of theatre which renders the real life story into a metaphorical framework, rather than to maintain a claim to complete authenticity. (p. 137)

Of course, ethnographic and verbatim theatre can produce very different types of audience experience, but the link here is the work with participants who may not be theatre professionals, who may have difficult stories to tell and whose lives the writer needs to protect and respect. There is still a lot of work that can be done in this area, however, and it is interesting to creatively explore these issues through performance and to use them as a very direct way of asking questions of the audience about the world we live in today. Both types of theatre often include a social or political issue or incident, however a potential pitfall can be the complete loss of theatrical story telling or entertainment value. During the writing of *Project XXX*, Paul Hine and I conducted research with groups of young people, discussing their ideas and experiences of Internet pornography, as we wanted to explore what effect the use of Internet porn could have on emotional relationships. We carried out research over many weeks and also worked very hard to ensure that the piece of theatre still had a good story to tell, that it was not just a theatrical presentation of a lot of facts, and that it provided value for money in terms of audience experience. With work like this it is often worth considering why this should be a play rather than a journalistic article for a Sunday supplement magazine. So, whilst we were working on a social issue with 'real' people, we chose not to go down the ethnographic or verbatim route because we felt that the subject matter needed to be fictionalised, that this was the more ethical as well as more theatrical route to go down. The ethics of verbatim and ethnographic theatre need to be very carefully considered before choosing this type of theatre practice, but more political work is touching upon these techniques and it is worth speculating on the methods used and creative possibilities of this type of theatre.

Fin Kennedy works a lot with non-theatre makers and non-professional actors in a London school to create new theatre work and suggests that this is another way to explore new possibilities in theatre making.

> **Fin Kennedy:** Mulberry School just opened their new space, a 150 seater theatre built on site, and they christened it with a sixteen-hander I wrote for them called *The Dream Collector*. When I write for teenagers, and particularly that school, there is such a lot of self-effacement that goes on. I am channelling those kids, and their fears and hopes and dreams, and I love doing that. I've done my best work at Mulberry School, but *The Dream Collector* was incredible. It is probably the sixth or seventh play I've written for the school and was by far the most challenging. They had to stage dreams, eight times. I didn't tell them they had to do it in the script, I just wrote this really rhythmic language, and they pulled it off brilliantly. And that really excites me. I say that without any subtext of ego, but theatre that excites me has that rawness to it, when people who

are not necessarily trained come to it, and become themselves through taking part in it – that really moves me.

Joe Sumsion also tells a story about working with actual people's lives, in a quite dramatic and potentially emotive situation, which new writers should learn from as his story illuminates the important work theatre can do as well as the importance of total respect for the people whose lives you are representing.

> **Joe Sumsion:** [I directed] a play called *The Bomb* by Kevin Dyer. It was commissioned at Action Transport and the play tells the story of the friendship between Pat McGee, who was the guy who planted the Brighton bomb, and Jo Berry, whose father was killed in the Brighton bombing. They met 20 years later and became friends of a sort. We commissioned a play to tell their story and they were involved with that. It was terrifying in a way, I remember the first day they came into rehearsals, two weeks into the process, and we showed them a run including part of the scene where they met for the first time. And this is the man who planted the bomb that killed her father, and this is still really raw, and something you want to get right, if there is a right. It was exciting because it felt as if we were doing something really important, and audiences got that. It is quite an amazing story, it is quite amazing that they would sit together in the same room and find a way to try to work together for peace, extraordinary really. It was one of those things where the more you look into it, the more dramatic it becomes, because the more you look into it, the more extraordinary it becomes. You have some plays and you think that is amazing, but then you explain and that takes some of that power away from it, but the more I thought about it, you know if I were her, how would I feel? So it was a brilliant play for empathy. A lot of theatre allows you to put yourself into the shoes of someone else, and those were very exciting and daunting shoes to jump into. *Could you meet the man who killed your father?* was the strapline on the poster.

That last question, that strapline, is incredibly emotive and yet the power of that story and the responsibility on the playwright is as enormous as it is exciting. The range of ways to explore new stories and new forms in theatre is one of the more creatively stimulating aspects of being a playwright. This is also perhaps the reason theatre is still relevant and still means so much to so many people. It is a medium that it is worth working in because the audience experience is live and can only come through a collaborative, creative experience, and theatre is the only place in which this combination can exist. Collaboration with the people whose stories you are telling is another part of this and often interests an audience, who can be drawn in by true-life stories, but I would underline again the need for respect when writing about people's actual lives. There have been as many disrespectful productions, sometimes by well-known companies, that purport to tell real-life stories, as there have been exciting and important productions. Ethnographic work always comes with this responsibility and need for respect.

Dramaturgs and dramaturgy

Part of the collaboration process that has come relatively recently to British theatre, having had a much longer history in Europe and the USA, concerns the role of the dramaturg and dramaturgy both in development and in productions, and this is something I will briefly explore before moving on to the next chapter.

The terms dramaturg and dramaturgy have been used often in this book so far, and they go back to Brechtian epic theatre. As Turner and Behrndt in their book *Dramaturgy and Performance* (2008) explain:

> Though the words are linked, 'dramaturgy' can be separated from the 'dramaturg': while the term 'dramaturgy' applies to the general composition of the work, the 'dramaturg' is a specific professional role. The 'dramaturgy' of a play or performance could also be described as its 'composition', 'structure' or 'fabric'. (p. 3)

So the term dramaturgy relates to the play not just on the page but also the way it is structured to tell the story in the best way possible. A good dramaturgical session should not consist of the dramaturg telling the playwright ways to change their play, although they may make suggestions. It is more about helping the playwright, and later the full creative team including the director, interrogate what is on the page and getting the playwright's ideas, vision and story across so that the 'instruction manual' is as clear to the creative team as it can be.

Turner and Behrndt also acknowledge that dramaturgs across Europe continue to debate what their role is within theatre, as there can be production dramaturgs who work in specific theatres whose role may be very different to the work of freelance dramaturgs, for example. Dramaturgy does not just happen on written plays either, it can be used for any type of performance, even any type of art, and is closely tied to the nature of collaborative creative work. Dramaturgy can be especially useful in devised work or performance work that is not necessarily traditional, site-specific theatre, for example or with new technologies. There are a few excellent books on dramaturgy, including the one cited here, and these can be found in the reading list at the back of this book. But it is important to note that the role of the dramaturg and the practice of dramaturgy is becoming more visible in British theatre now, and for new writers this gives another route for exploring practice and collaboration, as well as the space to push creative boundaries further in a safe environment.

Fin Kennedy spoke earlier about the need to 'self-dramaturg' as a playwright and Ruth Little, a freelance dramaturg, works across many art forms, not just with the written word, so there is a continual exploration in theatre and art of what this role means and what dramaturgs and dramaturgy can mean creatively. As collaboration is key to theatre making, and the dramaturg and dramaturgy key to collaborative working, the role and practice will hopefully continue to expand in British theatres over the next few years, providing emerging playwrights with new ways of developing and creating work.

10 New Voices, New Forms

In this chapter I want to further explore some of the challenges the digital age presents for theatre and think about what writers can do to continue to innovate creatively and make new work that speaks to our current cultural world. For example, how can a writer subvert traditional theatre writing and ensure that theatre is constantly evolving in a culture that often says it knows what it likes and it likes what it knows? Where can new playwrights take the form? How can cultural and theatrical experimentation be supported? Here is what Radosavljevic (2013) suggests, through an exploration of the work of Ontroedrend Goed, Tim Crouch and Silviu Purcrete:

> Despite generational, genealogical and cultural differences, all of these artists seem to have arrived at the idea that what was necessary in the first decade of the twenty-first century was for the proscenium arch to be removed and for the audience to be drawn into the inner workings of a theatre experience. (p. 4)

Whether this is still the case as we move into the second decade of the twenty-first century can be debated, but what is interesting in the work of these three very different artists is the ways in which they work with collaboration, whether that is with audiences, different artists and/or different art forms. Collaboration is a key theme of this book, so this chapter considers in more depth the ways new playwrights can bring their voice, a new voice, to theatre through innovative and exciting forms of collaboration.

Collaboration

For a variety of reasons, there seems to be a current trend of theatre makers to look for new ways to collaborate in creating new types of theatre productions.

A good example of this is a project I worked on recently, which was run by writers also acting as curators. Our aim was to produce new pieces of theatre all based on the concept of writers, directors and venues working collaboratively, rather than by the more traditional development and commission process. We set up six small scale productions in different venues across the North West of England. Over the year that this project took place, ten writer-curators worked with around another fifteen writers, six directors, and a number of actors, musicians and designers to create short runs of new plays. The project was an experiment, giving writers workshop time to get their short pieces redrafted and then giving them full productions. Each venue had a different theme, for example the short piece I wrote for The Dukes in Lancaster was a monologue by a mystical tramp-like figure and formed part of a linked narrative that took the audience around the backstage of the theatre in a type of site-specific promenade, where they met a host of interesting characters in unlikely places; the pieces I wrote for the show at The Royal Exchange in Manchester were created in collaboration with a DJ, and explored attitudes to youth and ethnicity through music. So whilst each writer created their own short plays, the majority of which were stand-alone pieces, the writing had to work within the whole performance and interact with the other short plays. This was not a group of writers working together on one play, although collaboration can work well like that, it was more about showcasing writing talent with individual pieces that were then curated into a greater whole. This project also worked in collaboration with the venues as the collective group of writers was funded through Arts Council England, meaning that whilst the venues were onboard and supportive, the producing of the shows was in the hands of the writers' collective.

The reason I explain this project is that it highlights a change in the way we can as writers produce theatre. Because producing theatres are reliant on subsidy through government funding, it is very difficult for these venues not to be reactive and work to a formula that is successful, in a bid to ensure that funding and support from the arts council is continued. However, there is always room for collaboration and playwrights can be at the heart of finding new ways to produce new work.

> **Joe Sumsion:** The current climate for theatre is hard. The Dukes is producing fewer of our own productions than we used to, there are more financial pressures on theatres. So here, the only way a writer would get their work on here is either that they just write the play themselves and send it in and it is so good, they get it through our script readers and we just have to put it on; or we commission them because there is a gap, so we have a park show or a Christmas show; or someone has an idea that is so compelling that we really think we have to have it because we really

feel it will really connect to our community. Writers can do a lot worse than really get to know a theatre well, get to know how that theatre works and thinks, because there is no point sending us a play that may be better suited to the ICA in London or the RSC because it has a cast of fifteen. We don't do big casts. Currently we are producing four plays a year, nearly all new writing, and this year that includes two co-productions, the Christmas show and the Park show. Then it is mostly touring work coming in. That seems to be the way of the world.

Our Young People's company work with new writers too; our creative learning department produces a lot of new work.

So my advice to writers would be to develop your own distinctive voice; you have to be determined and be prepared to draft and redraft and redraft. It is pragmatic as well – lots of successful writers have worked out how to get their plays on, and for younger writers that means not waiting for a professional company to produce you. Get it on, get it produced, by hook or by crook, and you're bound to learn from that experience.

Zosia Wand: Writers have to create opportunities for themselves now and that seems to be something that Arts Council England is encouraging. Although the decisions are not made by the theatre for that work then, the writer can go to the arts council and get their piece of theatre funded, and I'm not sure that's the right way around really. I think it is fine for workshopping but to actually put a play on, it seems to me that the initiative should come from the theatre. Currently I think writers have to be more proactive, we have to raise the money, we have to find the people to help us develop the work, we have to find creative ways around getting work produced, and it goes back to the idea that you must work on what you are passionate about.

Writers need to think simply, not just in terms of having to have a full-blown production, you can get just as much from a script in hand performance and a discussion night – work doesn't always have to go to full-scale production.

Of course, as Wand suggests, the ideal situation for all writers is that they are writing for the process, to create for the pleasure of creating the work, always finding new ways to write and learning from the work that has gone before. But I have already examined the difference between theatre writing and other types of writing, exploring the idea that creative collaboration and live performance are crucial to the final piece of work, meaning that many theatre makers do see a play on the page as 'wasted' if it does not get some form of production, if it simply stays on the page. Of course, with proper reflection all writing should be productive for the playwright in some way, but writing for the theatre means just that: the work will in some way be performed. And as mentioned above, with the current theatre climate changing, as Radosavljevic suggests, more directors, dramaturgs, performers and playwrights are blurring the lines between these different jobs:

> The notion of theatre-making implies a different model of the division of labour to the previously established ones which feature clearly delineated playwrights, directors, designers, producers and actors. In theatre-making the creative process seems to be more important than the formal division of labour itself. Similarly, the work's relationship with the audiences seems to be more important than any previously pursued hierarchies between text and performance. (p. 23)

Theatre has to remain relevant to the world around it through that live experience of the audience, otherwise you may as well be writing for films or digital adventure games. The story you make as a piece of theatre still needs to explore all the elements of what the 'theatrical' means, and this comes down to the presence of an audience.

> **Rob Drummer:** It is a live experience you are writing for. It is a room full of people who experience the work in real time, who made a journey and choice to come and sit in that room. You cannot pause it, you cannot walk out of it and return without having lost something, and many, many people will shape that experience. You can put the book down, you can pause the film, you can turn the volume up or down, with theatre you have to remember it is a room full of people who have committed to come together in that one place to spend the evening with your story at that one time. How you embrace, look after, challenge, provoke and immerse the audience is all the job of the playwright.

Theatre can engage the senses in a way no other form of writing yet can, as for example when Kevin Dyer spoke earlier about using real food in his plays because no other medium can use food in this way – the preparation, the eating, the smells. Earlier Billy Cowan mentioned the theatre company Quarantine, and I can recall going to see another one of their productions where the performers onstage made everyone in the (admittedly quite small) audience a cup of tea as part of the onstage action, which eased the audience into the storytelling world they were being invited to be a part of. As Holly Race Roughan, Steven Luckie, Joe Sumsion and Suzanne Bell also all point out, because theatre is live, as a writer you can ask your cast to interact with the audience, to stimulate their senses and to involve them in the creation of the piece of art that you began. Or as Chris Thorpe suggests, you can literally or metaphorically look your audience in the eye. So whilst the writing process is an end in itself for the writer, collaboration with the audience is crucial for a piece of theatre.

Collaborative writing

Collaborative writing can work in a couple of ways. It can be a show where two or more writers work together on one idea, one full length play for example, or it can be a production – like the project I mentioned above – which brings together several writers, each just writing short pieces that perhaps stand alone but are curated together into one production. This is not necessarily a new idea, but what it allows the writers to do is to work and learn from live production without needing a big single commission.

> **Ella Carmen Greenhill:** It is a huge risk for a company to produce just one play, but just having development and just having readings can really hold a writer up. I think the most helpful thing for writers is a production but it is a financial risk – so, for example *Wordplay*, by Box of Tricks Theatre Company, produced six 20 minute plays in a full production. This was not just a reading, the show had proper audiences, proper reviews and as a writer you had a proper production experience. You went through the same rehearsal process and you were treated as a writer in a full production, and this made you feel like a 'proper' writer. And now the theatre company is taking some of those pieces further.

Writers coming together to work collaboratively certainly spreads the risk for theatre companies and means that new networks can be formed and new ways of working can be found, whilst the writer still has the experience of a production. Learning to write to different lengths therefore becomes an important craft for a writer. In the Box of Tricks production, and in a similar way to the project I worked on, writers were given a short amount of time in which to tell a whole story. This could be analogous, if you're a prose writer, to creating flash fiction that can be published in magazines, building up a your writerly reputation whilst you work on your larger novel which takes a little more time and effort to get published. As a discipline and practice, writing short pieces works well, because it makes you as the writer think more concisely. You do not have space for reams of beautiful dialogue; you must be concise and structure the story in the best possible way for the timeframe you have. It helps form discipline for potential commissions, and means that you have to work to a type of brief but not one that is so structured it gives little room for creative manoeuvre, in the way some larger commissions can do. There is room for creative experimentation as an individual writer because the risk is spread across several writers. And all writers need to practice; as a writer you may believe that you are innovative, new and edgy, but work has to be seen by the audience to confirm that, and indeed the audience may support that view of your writing, or it may not. So this idea of the constant honing of your skills, not just in terms of the writing but also the performance, is an important one, and collaborations of writers give space for exactly that type of skill-honing through experimentation. What this can also mean is that your work is seen. As Rob Drummer and Lizzie Nunnery point out, writers can learn so much from other playwrights, not just well known ones, but emerging playwrights too.

> **Rob Drummer:** Playwrights should learn from each other. Writers coming together is important, exposing your work to other playwrights is very important. I think they can learn from established artists by seeing work live. Learning about theatre making rather than seeing writing as a literary endeavour is really important – see bad work as well as good work, go and see the work in the local community hall, if that is the closest place you have. I learn more about theatre from hating work than I ever do from being a big fan. Boy, how useful is it to come out of something and go: well that was just great! Critically you find it hard to then pull it apart.

> **Lizzie Nunnery:** I'm not really sure how anyone can be a playwright in isolation. Maybe there are people who can go off into the wilds and sit in a cottage and don't even visualise a particular theatre space, but that's never been the way I've worked. Obviously plays can take on a life the writer never imagined and make sense in all kinds of spaces to all kinds of audiences, but in terms of the actual process of crafting something, of starting and knowing how to see it through, I find it very useful to have a sense of who I'm writing for.

Writers can learn from other writers. I think new writers especially gain a lot by spending time in a room with other new writers having lots of conversations, because the process of how you actually put together a play is this ineffable thing that you can't solve. There's no answer to that question 'how do you write a play?' But the discussion of process and the links you can draw between the way you work and the way other people work, or the way other people work that you absolutely cannot – that can be incredibly helpful. I also think as playwrights we can learn from our younger selves. I heard

Frank Cottrell Boyce say once that he always reminds himself of the *play* part of writing plays and it really stuck with me. As children we play with stories unselfconsciously: we reel them out and discover them as we go and that's the fun of it. If we lose that sense of abandon and enjoyment there's a danger we won't be able to create that abandon and enjoyment for audiences.

The workshop process that often comes with a group of writers working together can also be a useful development tool for your writing, giving you the opportunity to learn from peers. This can be something as simple as reading each other's work on the page and giving feedback or bringing in friends or actors and having them read the work aloud. Of course, having your work performed means you can learn from an audience, and seeing the work of other writers in front of an audience can also be beneficial, because you learn the effect your words can have on that particular audience watching your story.

Lizzie Nunnery: New playwrights can learn from audience members. Seeing work and looking around you and listening to other people's conversations is invaluable. The best thing I ever did as a writer is really immersing myself in the Everyman and Playhouse in Liverpool, as buildings, as companies. I used to usher and do box office. I worked on stage door and later in the Literary Department, and I just went to see everything. I was in the Young Writer's group as well. Literally any way I could be inside the building I was going to be. I learnt so much from being amongst the company and being amongst the audience. You get a sense of what the ethos of that company is and whether you agree with it, but also what the demands of that community are. In the Everyman the audience have a particular personality. They're an audience that will stand up and walk out, or shout out, or laugh very loudly, or give a standing ovation – a demanding audience who want their money's worth, who want to feel something and think about something and really understand why they've seen the story they've just seen – to be delivered an ending that makes them feel they've been given some form of resolution. Sitting amongst that audience I knew I had to aim very high and I began to understand the sort of writer I wanted to be.

Theatre making

Collaborating as a writer with other theatre makers and perhaps becoming producer, or co-director, or working however you can on getting a production up and running, can be both creatively experimental and practically educational for the new playwright or theatre maker.

> **Ella Carmen Greenhill:** Producing yourself is quite a good thing to do as you see how hard it is, and sometimes as a writer it is quite easy to sit back and say, oh they're not putting on my work. But there are so many reasons, and so many ways a production is made that is it not just a case of waiting: go out there and do it. It is important to remember that every single person who is involved in your play, even if you disagree with what they are doing, will give everything to it, no one wants to make it bad – they may go off on a wrong route, or they do something in a different way to how you thought, and that is a conversation that needs to be had then with the company, but no wants to make your play rubbish, so you need to learn from that process.

Many playwrights have created or fronted their own theatre companies throughout the years, including John Godber (Hull Truck), Alan Ayckbourne (Stephen Joseph Theatre) and Brian Friel (Field Day Theatre Company) to name just a few. Noting this, it is interesting to consider why the idea still holds true for so many writers that to be good you must pass the 'gatekeepers', those directors, dramaturgs and literary associates who work in building-based theatres and who programme theatre seasons. Of course being commissioned or writing for the bigger theatres is important and a mark of success, however being passive and hoping one of these companies will produce you one day as long as you send them play after play after play is not necessarily the best way of learning about your craft as a writer or learning about making theatre.

And as I have already discussed, theatre priorities can change or move in a cyclical fashion. Radosavljevic points this out in relation to the way new writing in British theatre has risen and fallen in recent years:

> In the year 2010, the rise and rise of 'new writing' in the United Kingdom seemed to have arrived at an interesting point. At the beginning of the year *The Stage* newspaper reported that over the first decade of the twenty-first century, the amount of new writing in the subsidized sector had trebled, while a few months later producer Richard Jordan wrote in his column for the same publication that a similar trend was in evidence in London's West End too. Nevertheless, as the former article showed, there was also concern and dissatisfaction being expressed by British writers at the turn of the decade in response to the Arts Council's 'decision to remove new writing from its funding priorities in 2007'. (p. 85)

This change of priorities in 2007 meant that many of the independent script development agencies who had worked with new and established writers for around 30 years lost their funding from Arts Council England and new writing development fell to the producing houses in the regions. Whilst theatres became responsible for new writing, they did not necessarily have the funding or the ability to produce more new writing plays, because these companies also suffered cuts in their own funding.

Of course, it is not easy for writers to produce their own work either – it takes time, effort and often money. However as a student in a university, for example, there are often untapped resources in terms of venue space, peers who will work with you for free and ways of begging or borrowing costumes, props and sets. And if you are no longer a student, then get to know your local producing theatre, your local fringe theatres and your local amateur theatres. Learning from producing your own work may mean that you can build relationships with theatres who will see you being proactive and passionate about your work. And producing your work doesn't mean it has to be all singing and dancing – work can still be very simple and yet very theatrical.

> **Holly Race Roughan:** Theatre is more like writing for a gig than writing for a film, it is an understanding that you have to engage real people in real time in a real room. Even though we have moving lights, props and costumes and increasing use of video footage, the only real thing you have to fall back on, the backbone of every production, is the text. In cinema I've seen good films with not very good scripts, where the visual language is so strong, that you get something out of it in a different way, whereas that doesn't work in theatre.
>
> So, it is alive, it is immediate.
>
> Also you are writing something inherently poetic, you can sort of 'ish' put realism on stage, but it is a medium that allows you to do things like if you want to make the dad a chicken, you can make the dad a chicken, and that will go down in a way that just won't work on screen. What that allows you to do, to say about the world, to say about the dad, is mind-blowing, so for a writer the possibilities are endless. Whereas for TV and film, it is quite literal – so if the dad is a chicken, you have a problem on your hands. There are so many options for every story, it is incredibly exciting, it is a much bigger buffet for the imagination than screenwriting is. Not that is it superior, but it is a stadium for metaphor, and other art forms just don't work in the same way.

Producing yourself also allows you to be experimental with form, subject matter and audience experience. People are always hungry for new stories and new ways of telling those stories, but just because a new writer creates a family where the dad, to continue Race Roughan's idea, is a chicken does not inherently make this piece of theatre worth seeing. The crafting around the central concept that the father is a chicken is what is important, the understanding of the poetic aspects of theatre writing, the crafting of the dialogue and the ability to structure all of this into something an audience can both understand but at the same time forms questions or pushes them slightly to think more about the world they live in, all of this is what makes an exciting new piece of theatre.

> **Suzanne Bell:** The fundamental difference in writing for theatre is that it is live and it is active and it is a shared experience with many people; Dominic Dromgoole says that it is shared experience with not one but many critical minds, and you have to grab everyone. [...] In theatre you're watching characters make decisions live, in the moment, and they have a sense of time running out for them, they have a closing window of opportunity, a sense of danger if they don't make that decision, a sense of their own mortality, and a sense that once they step on a path, they can't undo that path. So there is a momentum behind theatre, or there needs to be, that an audience leans forward into. Also theatre is imaginative, it's not real, as much as you can try and create a sense of reality, it's not real. The playwright has made the decisions about who is going to say what to who, and how they're going to behave and how they're going to act, and why, and even if you create a set that is a realistic representation of life, it's not. So, use that imagination, use that audience's engagement with the imagination; I think audiences love that, because it reminds us of being children, and I think quite often we all just want to be kids again and be told a good story. I remember Noel Greig saying eight year olds are the best playwrights because they'll tell stories in the playground, and if the story isn't very good, everyone will just walk off, so they know they have to raise the stakes of the story, get to the ending, get to the punchline quite quickly. And that's theatre. And that's what audiences engage with.

To get this sense of the audience hearing your stories, and engaging with them live and in the moment, a play has to be produced. And the point raised by Greenhill above, that producing the work yourself not only gets that work out to an audience but also ensures the writer sees all sides of the process, is an important one. Understanding the practical issues of producing a show, understanding how to market a show, especially through digital and social media platforms, and learning then to read the audience watching your show, can be much more valuable than simply sending a play out to 30 or 40 theatres and hoping that one of them will produce it. Do still send out your plays, of course, but also be proactive in terms of ways of getting your work to an audience, no matter how small the venue. It may also help you find different ways of working and you could find that in fact you prefer to direct, dramaturg or produce, either instead of or as well as writing. As Nunnery said above, playwrights cannot work in isolation, they have to collaborate; who to collaborate with and how to collaborate on that piece of theatre can be as creatively satisfying as simply writing your play and sending it off.

Collaboration with other artists

Another form of collaboration is the process known as devised theatre, which is a term you may have heard a few times in this book already, and can also be known as workshopping.

In Part 1, Zosia Wand spoke of her admiration for Max Stafford-Clarke, who, through several theatre companies, would work with actors and often a playwright, such as Mark Ravenhill, to create a play may only be written, in the traditional sense, after a 'rehearsal' process. Mike Leigh and Joan Littlewood are two other directors who worked with this process. It has interesting implications for the playwright, who becomes part of a creative team who are making a piece of theatre rather then the initiator, although the idea for the story may originate with the writer. So there are pluses and minuses to this process. On the plus side, there is the creative experimentation and the creative spark that can only happen in a team. On the minus side, the playwright does not 'own' the work perhaps so much as she or he does when working alone.

Radosavljevic (2013) suggests that devising as a term only came about in Britain in the latter part of the twentieth century, and that it was a popular tool in 'political theatre, community theatre, theatre in education (TIE), performance art' (p. 59) as well as for those companies like Stafford-Clarke's who were exploring different ways of working. She goes on to say:

> On balance, a departure from the term 'devising' in contemporary theatre and performance discourse may well be wise, not least because of the fact that its apparent inflation in the United Kingdom has led to a number of misconceptions. Firstly, its implied binary opposition to text-based theatre tends to create confusion among continental Europeans, as work on any pre-written text in many European mainstream theatres customarily

involves a collective and an improvisational approach in the process of rehearsal. [...] In the twenty-first century context of increasingly globalized theatre-making, we must recognize that the divide between text-based theatre and devised performance is no longer tenable. (p. 62)

However, I would suggest that this is more of an academic view and that experiments with devising pieces, collaborating with actors, directors and designers to create a piece, whilst a luxury for many writers (as it can be an expensive process with everyone involved needing to be paid) is still a useful tool for the writer in developing a piece for performance. Practically, then, devising as a form of collaboration with other artists is, and continues to be, a recognised form of working, whether this means that the writer goes with a director into a working space with some actors and tries out some improvised ideas around a basic concept before writing the play, or the whole piece is devised and the creative team, including the writer, make the piece together. Movements and trends in creative practice cannot be historicised in clear cut chunks of time; they overlap and pop up or disappear in a seemingly random fashion. Devising as a form of collaborative theatre making has been around for some time, but I do not get a sense that in practice it is quite dead yet, even if as a term it is not useful in critical discourse around theatre.

Collaboration with other art forms

In Chapter 8 I considered some innovations in theatre that are happening now, and who the innovators of the future might be, and one of those artists, suggested by Rob Drummer, was Sabrina Mahfouz, an emerging writer who works across different platforms, including performance poetry, storytelling and using music. Drummer sees her as being an important innovator because of the work she does with other artists as well as her writing. Of course, mixing art forms in theatre has always happened, even in the Renaissance, when playwrights wrote in verse and were considered poets, and when the balladeers contributed to the sense of Renaissance theatre in terms of entertainment with lurid, almost gossip-like, retelling of stories to excite, appall and pull in the crowd. So whilst it is clear that theatre revolves around a dialogic form of storytelling, in that it uses dialogue between characters and also a dialogue between those on stage and the audience, what is also clear is that this does not exclude other art forms from being involved in that storytelling. Many theatre companies are currently exploring how to use different types of art form to create new ways to tell a story. For example, a 2013 tour of *Melody Loses Her Mojo* by the young people's theatre company Twenty Stories High, based in Liverpool, used hip hop music, a cellist and puppetry to tell the story of the young protagonist Melody. So for a young teenage audience the play was a relevant piece of theatre that spoke to them because, for example, they could empathise with Melody as a character through the music she has around her, similar to the type of music they might listen to. But in terms of the form of the play, Melody's little sister, who is aged four, and whom the story revolves around, can be portrayed through a puppet, adding that element of magic to the relationship between the two siblings and heightening the reality of the story they are telling, whilst at the same time answering a practical issue of having a four year old on stage.

Of course, the art form that has perhaps dominated this part of the book is digital art or technology.

The use of film or video in theatre performance has been around for a while, and it is not what I mean by 'digital'. I have already explored the idea that it is a medium that threatens the live, shared experience when the thorny issue of having to leave your house and pay loads of money to risk watching something that may be dull when you can stay at home and watch YouTube is always there. But there are ways of utilising these new forms of technology and writers can consider the variety of ways digital technology is affecting audiences, in terms of concentration and expectation.

Rob Drummer: It is structural; I am less and less interested in reading plays about the digital age. Lots of people sat onstage typing away. I am much more interested how form online is completely uncharted. You get eleven minute episodes of continuing drama on YouTube, you can download an episode of something on iPlayer and watch it whenever you want, there are increasingly shows being premiered on iPlayer, you can watch the new *House of Cards* adaptation all in one go over 24 four hours on Netflix, and this does something specific to an audience. There is greater agency for the audience, and if theatre is going to respond it will have to start responding through form, start responding through structure, start looking at how stories are being digested by an audience and grab that opportunity. This is what Caryl Churchill is doing in *Love and Information,* she wants to write a play about people, relationships and too much unfiltered information in our digital, so the only form that work can take for her is through a series of scenes with around 100 characters played by an ensemble, a series of short, snappy, completely unrelated parts that add up to something that feels intoxicating; and that is a piece of work about the digital age as far as I'm concerned. Never does the piece talk about the digital, but it could only be made by it, it could only be written now as it is influenced by how stories are told. That is more interesting than writing about how it is to be 14 and watching videos on YouTube. Our attention spans are different as well. *Disgraced* by Ayad Akhtar is structured in a very filmic way; set up, story and resolution, because we understand the way film structure works, so why shouldn't theatre steal from these more popular forms? You have a 90 minute play that an audience get because they have watched films like this. Lots of theatre makers and critics might say but that's not good theatre because it is not necessarily well made or doesn't follow the rules, but what are those rules and why can't they be broken always? I think it is formal, I think it is structural and I think theatre then starts to be part of a wider culture of contemporary storytelling, otherwise doesn't it stay trapped behind the proscenium starting to gather dust?

Instead of simply portraying digital technology, or using the term multimedia to describe your work because you have included some music and video, Drummer believes that the actual form of what we are watching on these ever changing digital platforms is something theatre writers should start exploring through theatre plays. Playwrights can explore ways of using screenwriting structure; for example, I mentioned in Part 1 that looking at screenwriting craft texts can be useful for the playwright when playing around with structural exercises, and using something like Snyder's beat sheet (2005) or Batty's 'tent-poles' (2008) and applying this to a stage piece can be interesting because it is a structure an audience used to Hollywood films will immediately get. Now, I'm not suggesting every piece of theatre should work like a screenplay structurally, but it is another tool to use when exploring form. The idea of digital form also links to the use of short pieces and of collaborative work, as well as the comment Race Roughan made earlier about theatre being more like a gig than a film. We have to consider the audience expectations and how these have changed over the last few decades. Thinking back to the theatre history chapter in Part 1 of this book, theatre has lasted at least 2,500 years, but playwrights have to consider that it is only in the last 150 years that a series of technological advances have changed the way Western society lives, and therefore changed not only the way theatre is viewed, but the way theatre relates to society. Electricity, photography, film, radio and television all played their part in this technological revolution, and indeed most of these were heralded as sounding the death knell for theatre; likewise, digital technology is supposedly posing the same threat, but instead a lot of new theatre is being made.

Ruth Little: [Digital technology] sits in tension with [theatre] – the tension between embodied and disembodied experience. Theatre is also an exploration of mind in the crucible space of the stage – symbolic, articulate, intentional – and digital technology can enhance or support that inner exploration. It can tease the eye and ear (for example through binaural technology). It can also generate reach and greater access, allow to some extent for expanded collaboration. Too often though it's either emotionally or narratively illustrative, though I think there's huge scope still for animation in relation to moving bodies and objects. And it's important to remember that theatre came out of another 'digital' age – when the human hand was the primary tool for making and self-expression, and theatre reminds us that the raw human body is our primary means of experiencing the world and making meaning out of it. I think digital technology can extend the capacities of the body, and it's worth exploring that in relation to both performer and audience, but now more than ever we need to renew and deepen our understanding of the capabilities and frailties of the human body, and bring notions of agency and responsibility back 'home', as it were.

So whilst it is important to begin to acknowledge and find new ways of working with technology in what is loosely being called 'the digital age', that is from the start of the new millennium, what all the theatre makers I interviewed were clear about was that:

- Theatre is a live experience, and whilst innovations like NT Live are useful, they do not replace live theatre.
- Digital technology and multimedia is more than writing about Twitter and Facebook and projecting some video material onto a screen.
- There will be new ways of theatre interacting with digital technologies, but these will not replace the live experience of theatre.

> **Joe Ward Munrow:** We're really lucky because you can't pirate theatre. We are lucky that our audiences have to be there, they can't take it away for free, but people who make films or TV, I do wonder where their income will come from in the next 20 years. People are getting used to having art and music for free, so I think in theatre we are really lucky. I've no desire to use screens or technology, I like the fact that theatre is timeless. Theatre will have a resurgence, as screens and smart phones become ubiquitous and everything we see is pre-recorded or is 2-D. Going out will become odd, it will be more of an experience to go out and sit with people in a room and see real people on stage. Not that it will become freaky, but we will notice that it will be a qualitatively different experience to screens and information on tap. The real live experience will become more appealing, more enticing. I hope that will be what happens.

Collaboration with digital technology is not simply a matter of utilising social media or film or other forms within the piece, and it is not necessarily about writing about the digital age, but it is about that collaboration with technology and allowing that into the very forms and structures of the work we are writing. In a project Ella Carmen Greenhill and I worked on with four other writers at the Royal Exchange in Manchester we set writers the task of writing short plays in collaboration with a musician that lasted exactly the length of a song. Each of the six writers wrote three pieces, some linked and some did not, and whilst we were not writing 'about' the digital age, and whilst we did not use screens or film, we were engaging and collaborating with other art forms and the digital age in terms of form and structure; these were short pieces of theatre, and whilst the live element of not being able to pause or switch off was there, the shortness of the pieces involved meant that, like a YouTube clip or a live gig, if an audience member did not like that particular piece, there was always another one along a few minutes later.

Of course not all theatre has to be made like this, there will always be room for the commissioned piece of work, the children's show, the adaptation and the play that speaks to the location of the theatre and the community the theatre serves. The point here is that, despite the digital age giving everyone a screen in their pocket on which they can watch whenever they want, a lot of new theatre is still being made, and it is engaging and collaborating with the world around it, and to survive this is perhaps something new playwrights need to acknowledge also.

> **Chris Thorpe:** It's not so much about where does theatre fit in the digital age, it's more where does the digital age find its comfortable place to be in theatre? It's not about theatre going out there and trying to compete with all these other art forms that don't need this room and this presence.
>
> Yes, you can document theatre digitally; yes, you can put it out there interactively; yes you can find performances that really successfully combine the world outside and inside the theatre by digital means – but theatre doesn't have to go out there and say we need to find our digital equivalent or our digital niche. Theatre and the digital world, which are not mutually exclusive, need to look at each other and go, what are the elements of both of these things that can fight with each other or reinforce each other, or go to be together?
>
> It kind of suggests that theatre has been somehow superseded by the digital age, and it has not; the digital age is a thing that has happened in the world

in the same way the bronze age happened, in the same way that commu-nism happened, in the same way that any paradigm shift in the world hap-pens, and there's been theatre all the way through those things. So it is not more inherently difficult for theatre to communicate with people in the digital world than it was in a pre-digital world. It is about saying – 'Theatre, what excites you about the digital world? Go and have a chat about that'.

11 Speculative Exercises and Key Points

There are many ways of creating new theatre, with collaboration and interaction with other art forms being key. What follows is a series of exercises that can help the emerging playwright enter into a dialogue with the text, with the aim of pushing theatre writing in new directions and taking work out to a new audience. At the end of this chapter there is also a section on where to go for development opportunities, theatres who have a new writing remit and potential funding sources. Obviously this list will change constantly, so again it should be seen as a starting point for your own further research.

As before in Chapter 6, some of these exercises will come from the interviewees, and as such will be credited to them. Exercises can be collaborative or sole exercises, and it will be indicated whether they are intended for use on actual plays that the writer is currently working on or whether they are purely creative practice.

Exercise 1: Pitching (collaborative exercise – creative practice)

In a group of three or four, create a pitch specifically designed for a theatre in your area. Research the kind of work that this theatre produces already and include in your pitch a discussion of where the theatre might be missing new audiences. If you are in a classroom or writing group situation, present this to the wider group and encourage questions. Think about how you would collaborate to write such a piece of theatre, how you might produce it and how you might market it for those new audiences.

Exercise 2: Awareness (sole exercise – creative practice)

> **Ruth Little:** I encourage writers to walk and record their walks – not necessarily in words – to develop attention and begin to look at patterns and their disruption, at labour, ritual, the many forms of communication at play between people. And to pay attention to light, sound, colour, form – to

think beyond the sometimes neutral and malleable space of the studio or the more prescriptive but rather self-referential space of the proscenium arch stage. I remember the impact of the end of Sarah Kane's *4.48 Psychosis* in James MacDonald's production upstairs at the Royal Court – when the actors opened the big windows onto Sloane Square, and light and sound bled in, with the ordinary lives of people outside who were unaware that they were 'in' the play, and what a beautiful and humane and encompassing gesture that was.

Exercise 3: Sensory (sole exercise – working on a play)

Kevin Dyer: This is something I do: I have a bag of coloured materials, some are sparkly, some are dull, some are brown, red ones, green ones, big ones, little ones, shiny ones – whatever. And if I'm working on a character arc I look at all of them and I find one that is the character at a critical part of their story. So I put my hand in this pile of material and find one that is deep, deep red, and that's not what the character is wearing, but what they are inside at a point of the story. That's them when their wife's been arrested for soliciting – that's how they feel. Then I will find another piece for before or after that moment, I might find, let's say, a white piece of material at the moment when they find out that their wife is and has been cheating on them for 20 years, and that's the moment when they feel numb and completely lost. And then I'll find a third piece from another part of the story, and this might be the end of the story when they realise that it has all been a set up, it is all lies, and that actually this man's wife is something else. So just finding three colours gives me three very different visual stages of the story. For me, all the time, I look for visual ways of showing how characters feel at stages of their journey.

And you can use material, colours or objects. You know – at the beginning of the story my character might be a grain of sugar, at another point they might be a cream cake, at another stage they might be a lamb roast. You know, use those visual things, those non-brain things. Plays are complicated, and they can really do your head in, so I try to find ways of simplifying the play. Make it simple, make it simple, make it simple. But I am still working it out, all the time, how to write a play.

Exercise 4: Objects (collaborative exercise – creative practice)

Ruth Little mentioned using this exercise, and it is also something I do with my students. Working in a group of about 10 to 15 writers, each brings to the workshop an object that has particular significance to them. The writer presents the object to the group and explains in about five minutes why the object is important. In pairs, writers then swap their objects and write short scenes around them, which can be read out later if appropriate. This exercise has several purposes: firstly, it can focus the mind on something other than just trying to create action or conflict through character; secondly, it can help communication between writers, aiding collaborative work further down the line; finally, the focus on the story within the object can be used by the writer and expanded on, giving the writer a springboard to create from.

Exercise 5: Unblocking (sole exercises – working on a play)

> **Elizabeth Newman:** The Vicar's Suitcase – This is my vicar's suitcase and in it I have a hat, an umbrella, a table, a chair, a frog, a dog, a wibbly worm, a plant, a planet, stars, Venus, moon, Earth, the sound of waves, my mother, my father, my husband – you just list a load of things quickly that could be in the suitcase and a load of words fall out, and it can be really useful to unblock.

> Raffle Tickets – write down all the different senses, words that you associate with those senses, onto raffle tickets, then keep them in a pot – you can ask other people to write these down too – and if you get blocked, just pick out a raffle ticket.

Exercise 6: Improvise/devise (collaborative exercise – creative practice or working on a play)

Working with form can be difficult, and of course the advice to read as many current plays as possible is the best advice anyone can give a new playwright, but you can also play with form in creative practice. This next exercise can be both useful and fun if you have never written a play before, but it is also useful if you need to move a draft on.

In pairs, create a basic idea for a play, with two characters, basic storyline (who wants what from whom) and theme. Two more people (either actors or writers, but I will refer to them as actors for the rest of the exercise) then join the two writers and take their place in an acting area (although there should be no audience for this). The writers each instruct the actors about the scene they would like them to improvise, giving them the basic story, each character's motivations and the ending of the scene. This can be recorded or filmed if everyone agrees. The actors then improvise the scene until the writers ask them to stop. The actors can now have a short break whilst the writers write up the scene, combining elements from the improvisation, elements that they originally wanted in the scene and new elements that may have come up through the improvisation. The actors can then come back and read the scene for the larger group.

This exercise can be done over a two hour workshop as practice, but over a period of days or even weeks when writing a play.

Exercise 7: Art forms (sole exercise – creative practice or working on a play)

Write a scene. Now start to think about how you might involve other art forms, for example:

- Change one of the characters into a puppet.
- Change one of the characters into a digital entity only – a hologram for example.
- Change the dialogue of one of the characters so that they only speak in verse or in rhyme, or in noises that are not actual words.
- Swap one of the characters for a musical instrument.
- Swap one of the characters for an inanimate object.

There may be other swaps you can think of doing, but keep changing these elements within the play and be mindful of what this is doing to the form of the play or the scene.

Exercise 8: Patience (sole exercise – working on a play)

Rob Drummer Finding the heart of your story:

Upon completion of your first full draft of the play, walk away from it, leave it, don't give it another thought and only when you cannot bear it come back to the play and read with fresh eyes. Read it in one sitting and without distraction then put it down and write a story synopsis, a paragraph long, detailing the whole story of your first draft (which might be different to the play you thought you were writing). Now read this and start again, limiting yourself to two sentences, then repeat and give yourself a sentence. Step away and notice what of the story you have omitted already and then reduce the sentence to five words, then three and finally a single word. Read back through all of these and observe where, for you, the heart of the story lies, it is often in the sentence, definitely in the single word and will be the perfect exercise in returning to the play ahead of the second draft.

Exercise 9: Secrets and lies (sole exercise – working on a play)

Rob Drummer: If you are struggling with a scene that feels as if it is lacking dramatic action or with a character who is becoming representative of an idea rather than possessing real depth then consider investing in secrets and lies.

Extract a scene from your play (or equally start with a basic character building exercise) and look at two of the characters, who might have little interaction with each other. What happens when you bury a secret between them and introduce a third character or better still a secret that has fuelled a lie told to protect another character.

Try by inserting a lie into the dialogue:

A: *I didn't leave the house at all yesterday.*

B: *Not at all?*

A: *I couldn't could I, I had to wait for the delivery.*

B: *Funny because Simon said he saw you.*

Ok, so it is a crude example but you get the point – instantly a lie becomes a way of increasing the dramatic tension and heightening the stakes between two characters. Quickly a lie could escalate and come back to impact later in the play.

My favourite sort of play is the family drama and it is no great secret that most great examples (I am thinking *August: Osage County* by Tracy Letts, *Buried Child* by Sam Shepard, *The Herd* by Rory Kinnear) thrive upon buried secrets in the past that detonate mid way through the play and must be worked through to reach any sense of resolution.

If you are struggling with a character, then why not invest in backstory and bury a secret, something that is slowly weathering the character from the inside, an act committed years ago that only one other person knows about and then, at the start of the second scene, that person enters.

The final exercise in this section is more of a research project. As in Exercise 1, you should keep a note of what types of shows your local theatre is producing, but also look at theatre companies mentioned by the interviewees in this book, look up the work of those interviewed and begin to explore how and where your work might fit in. Remember, do not necessarily tailor your work specifically to fit: as many of the directors, writers and dramaturgs here have said, if your work is good, it will find a home and you must write what you want to write, what you are passionate about. However, beginning the research project of discovering where your work might fit is a good starting point, and below is a list of websites, theatres and literary departments that might be able to help you or theatre companies you can look to simply for more inspiration. Keep a file, notebook or spreadsheet with this info and make sure you go back to it at least once a week. You can make a note of your progress with particular companies or projects, and this can be useful for further writing reflection.

Where to go next?

These types of lists can often fall out of date quickly (indeed during the editing stage, one of the organisations I had listed disappeared!) so I have attempted to be as broad as possible with this list of organisations and theatres currently useful for playwrights to know about.

Arts Council England – http://www.artscouncil.org.uk/

This is the main funding organisation in England for those wanting to create their own productions. Grants for the Arts is the current stream for individual artists or small organisations and full details of how to apply and where to get advice are available on the website.

Arts Council of Northern Ireland – http://artscouncil-ni.org

This is the funding and development agency for arts in Northern Ireland.

Arts Council of Wales – http://www.artswales.org.uk

The Welsh arts council can also fund and advise artists who are living and creating work in Wales.

Creative Scotland – http://www.creativescotland.com

This organisation incorporates what was Arts Council Scotland, proving funding, resources and advice for a range of arts and creative industries in Scotland.

BBC Writers Room – http://www.bbc.co.uk/writersroom/

Perhaps more thought of as a resource for those wanting to write TV and radio but they do read theatre scripts when the submission windows are open and can give very useful feedback for theatre writers.

Playwrights Studio Scotland – http://playwrightsstudio.co.uk

For Scottish playwrights, a development agency for writers at all levels.

New Writing North – http://www.newwritingnorth.com/writers-writing-for-theatre-page-1438.html

This is a development agency which highlights opportunities across the country.

The Playwrights Studio, Glasgow – http://www.playwrightsstudio.co.uk/

This organisation helps to develop playwrights, primarily in Scotland.

The British Theatre Guide – http://www.britishtheatreguide.info/

This website has a lot of info about what theatre is on and where, including reviews and previews.

The theatres listed below all have some new writing remit and more info can be found on their websites as not all will necessarily accept unsolicited scripts. And if I have not included your local theatre, please do not think this is because they are not interested in new writing, simply check them out yourself. There are new theatres and theatre companies being created all the time, so as with all the advice in this book, please do use these lists as the springboard for your own research. But note: firstly, always read the new writing submission policy, and secondly, some theatres really do not have the resources to read through a lot of scripts, so always contact the theatre first and ask rather than sending your work and hoping for the best.

Theatre 503 – https://theatre503.com/

The Bush – http://www.bushtheatre.co.uk/

The Octagon, Bolton – http://www.octagonbolton.co.uk/home

The Liverpool Everyman and Playhouse – http://www.everymanplayhouse.com/

The Royal Court, London – http://www.royalcourttheatre.com/

The Royal Exchange, Manchester – http://www.royalexchange.co.uk/page.aspx

Most of the new writing at The Royal Exchange goes via The Bruntwood Prize, info for which can be found here: http://www.writeaplay.co.uk/

The Dukes, Lancaster – http://www.dukes-lancaster.org/

Contact Theatre, Manchester – http://contactmcr.com/

Birmingham Rep – http://www.birmingham-rep.co.uk/

Traverse Theatre, Scotland's New Writing Theatre – http://www.traverse.co.uk/

Papatango – http://papatango.co.uk/

Paines Plough – http://www.painesplough.com/home

Hampstead Theatre – http://www.hampsteadtheatre.com/playwriting/

Soho Theatre – http://www.sohotheatre.com/

The Finborough Theatre, London – http://www.finboroughtheatre.co.uk/about.php

Theatre Royal, Plymouth – http://www.theatreroyal.com/about-us/our-work/information-for-writers/

The following theatres may not have such a clear new writing remit, but if they are in your area you may want to contact them to begin a relationship if you consider your work to be beyond the developmental stage, or they may have a youth theatre or community theatre company you can access:

Nottingham Playhouse – http://nottinghamplayhouse.co.uk

Watford Palace – http://watfordpalacetheatre.co.uk

Home, Manchester – http://homemcr.org/theatre/

Derby Theatre – http://derbytheatre.co.uk

Mercury Theatre, Colchester – http://mercurytheatre.co.uk

York Theatre Royal – http://yorktheatreroyal.co.uk

Queens Theatre, Hornchurch – http://queens-theatre.co.uk

Arcola Theatre, London – http://arcolatheatre.com

Citizens Theatre, Glasgow – http://citz.co.uk

Salisbury Playhouse – http://salisburyplayhouse.com

Theatre by the Lake, Keswick – http://theatrebythelake.co.uk

Live Theatre, Newcastle – http://live.org.uk

National Theatre Scotland – http://nationaltheatrescotland.com

National Theatre Wales – http://nationaltheatrewales.org

Abbey Theatre, Dublin – http://abbeytheatre.ie

Gate Theatre, Dublin – http://gatetheatre.ie

Corcadorca, Cork – http://theatredevelopmentcentre.com

Theatre Clwyd, Mold – http://clwyd-theatr-cymru.co.uk

Lyric Theatre, Belfast – http://lyrictheatre.co.uk

The following theatre companies and festivals may have competitions or work on that can inspire you:

The Unity Theatre, Liverpool – http://www.unitytheatreliverpool.co.uk

Tamasha Theatre Company – http://www.tamasha.org.uk/home/

Box of Tricks Theatre Company – http://www.boxoftrickstheatre.co.uk/

Tinderbox Theatre – http://www.tinderbox.org.uk/about-us/

Hull Truck Theatre Company – http://www.hulltruck.co.uk/open-space/new-writing

Action Transport – http://www.actiontransporttheatre.org/

High Tide Festival – http://www.hightide.org.uk/

247 Festival, Manchester – http://www.247theatrefestival.co.uk/

Pilot Theatre Company – http://www.pilot-theatre.com/

Fuel Theatre Company – http://fueltheatre.com

Kneehigh Theatre Company – http://www.kneehigh.co.uk/

Shared Experience Theatre – http://www.sharedexperience.org.uk/

The Sphinx Theatre Company – http://www.sphinxtheatre.co.uk/

Out of Joint Theatre Company – http://www.outofjoint.co.uk/

A final word of advice on social media

In this second section of the book, I have spoken a lot about this being the digital age and about social media and digital platforms. Social media as tools for networking and marketing are incredibly useful and fast becoming a vital form of PR for both yourself as a writer and your work. Links to other writers and theatre companies will help you with opportunities and potential collaborations. But a word of caution, which may be obvious to some (if so, apologies) but which is something I have often encountered: if you use social media professionally, do not use the same social media to upload photos of your tea, your dog, you drunk (or worse...). If you want a professional relationship with that person or company, you have to work hard at keeping it that way, and mistakes can easily be made. Either create separate personal and professional profiles or be very wary of what you post. Also, be very aware of your own Internet profile. If you have a blog or a website, update it regularly and don't make wild claims that have only the most tenuous grasp on reality! Publicity is important, but you are going to be carrying this profile around with you for what will hopefully be a long and successful career, so at the start of it try to ensure that what you post at 20 won't come back to haunt you at 40.

Conclusion to Part 2

The aim of this book is to help the emerging playwright think more about why they might want to write for theatre. By interviewing some of this century's key playwrights, directors and dramaturgs, the aim has been to include the new writer in a world that may at first seem a little alien. Hopefully, the world of writing for theatre seems more solid now and less nebulous. But there will always be a certain nebulous quality to writing for theatre due to that live aspect, which can see a group of people devoting weeks of their lives to a particular piece, only for it to disappear after the run has finished and to exist only in the memories of those who worked on it and those who watched it. And that is the beauty of theatre. There may be a published playscript or a film of a performance somewhere, but that live moment has gone forever. This is why writers of theatre are often much more involved in the production of their work than any other type of writer, because they know it will all disappear and we will simply be left with that poster or that book or those few photos. Embrace the nebulous aspect and be willing to collaborate and creatively explore what you can do in the theatre space and use it to tell the story that only you can tell. That is the final message this book has for you, the new playwright.

Further Reading

Firstly, here is a list of plays that would be useful for any emerging playwright to read. And again, this list is in no way definitive. Some of these plays will have been published in many editions, so it doesn't really matter which edition you get hold of – what matters is that you get a sense of how the playwright works. Many of those listed have written more than the one or two plays I mention here; once you've read one of their plays, research their other work, and remember: just keep reading as much as you can.

These are in author surname order and include the published work of the playwrights interviewed for this book.

Aeschylus – *The Oresteia*

Edward Albee – *Who's Afraid of Virginia Woolf?*

April de Angelis – *Playhouse Creatures*

Anonymous – *Everyman*

Aristophanes – *Lysistrata*

James Baldwin – *The Amen Corner*

Howard Barker – *Scenes From An Execution*

Peter Barnes – *The Ruling Class*

Mike Bartlett – *Earthquakes in London*

Samuel Beckett – *Happy Days*

Samuel Beckett – *Waiting for Godot*

Aphra Behn – *The Rover*

Alan Bennett – *Talking Heads*

Alecky Blythe – *Little Revolution*

Edward Bond – *Saved*

Bertolt Brecht – *Mother Courage*

Bertolt Brecht and Kurt Weil – *The Threepenny Opera*

Gregory Burke – *Blackwatch*

Leo Butler – *Lucky Dog*

Jez Butterworth – *Jerusalem*

Ella Carmen Greenhill – *Plastic Figurines*

Jim Cartwright – *Road*

Anton Chekov – *read as many of his plays as you can get your hands on!*

Caryl Churchill – *Far Away*

Caryl Churchill – *Love and Information*

Caryl Churchill – *Top Girls*

William Congreve – *The Way Of The World*

Billy Cowan – *Still Ill*

Martin Crimp – *Attempts On Her Life*

Tim Crouch – *The Author*

Shelagh Delaney – *A Taste Of Honey*

Ariel Dorfman – *Death and the Maiden*

Kevin Dyer – *The Bomb*

David Edgar – *Playing With Fire*

Kevin Elyot – *My Night With Reg*

Euripides – *The Trojan Women*

Vivian Franzmann – *Mogadishu*

Michael Frayn – *Copenhagen*

Brian Friel – *Faith Healer*

Brian Friel – *Translations*

John Gay – *The Beggar's Opera*

Debbie Tucker Green – *Born Bad*

David Greig – *The Strange Undoing of Prudencia Hart*

Lee Hall – *Cooking With Elvis*

Lorraine Hansberry – *A Raisin In The Sun*

David Hare – *Pravda*

David Harrower – *Blackbird*

Tom Holloway – *Red Sky Morning*

Henrik Ibsen – *again, read as many of his plays as possible, but definitely read A Doll's House*

Eugene Ionesco – *The Chairs*

Alfred Jarry – *Ubu Roi*

Ben Jonson – *Volpone*

Sarah Kane – *Blasted*

Dennis Kelly – *Love and Money*

Charlotte Keatley – *My Mother Said I Never Should*

Fin Kennedy – *Protection*

Ayub Khan-Din – *East is East*

Tony Kushner – *Angels in America*

Bryony Lavery – *Frozen*

Dan LeFranc – *The Big Meal*

Lorca – *Blood Wedding*

Sharman MacDonald – *When I Was A Girl I Used To Scream And Shout*

Duncan Macmillan – *Monster*

David Mamet – *Oleanna*

Christopher Marlowe – *Faustus*

Martin McDonath – *The Lieutenant of Inishmore*

Menander – *Dyskolos or The Grouch*

Arthur Miller – *read as many of his plays as you can, but definitely Death of a Salesman and All My Sons*

Molière – *The Misanthrope*

Chloe Moss – *This Wide Night*

Anthony Neilson - *The Wonderful World Of Dissocia*

Lizzie Nunnery - *Intemperance*

Sean O'Casey - *Juno and the Paycock*

Joe Orton - *Entertaining Mr Sloane*

Joe Orton - *What The Butler Saw*

John Osborne - *Look Back In Anger*

John Osborne - *The Entertainer*

Harold Pinter - *read all of his plays, especially The Caretaker, The Birthday Party, Betrayal*

Luigi Pirandello - *Six Characters In Search Of An Author*

Plautus - *Bacchides*

Stephen Poliakoff - *Blinded by the Sun*

Dennis Potter - *Brimstone and Treacle*

Lucy Prebble - *Enron*

Terrence Rattigan - *The Deep Blue Sea*

Mark Ravenhill - *Some Explicit Polaroids*

Philip Ridley - *Pitchfork Disney*

Willy Russell - *Educating Rita*

Peter Shaffer - *Equus*

William Shakespeare - *any of his plays*

George Bernard Shaw - *Mrs Warren's Profession*

Sam Shepard - *Fool For Love*

Martin Sherman - *Bent*

Sophocles - *The Theban Plays*

Simon Stephens - *Motortown*

Simon Stephens - *Port*

Tom Stoppard - *Rosencrantz and Guildenstern Are Dead*

August Strindberg - *Miss Julie*

J. M. Synge – *The Playboy Of The Western World*

Terence – *The Brothers*

Chris Thorpe – *There Has Possibly Been An Incident*

Lawrence Till and Barry Hines – *Kes*

Laura Wade – *Breathing Corpses*

Enda Walsh – *Disco Pigs*

John Webster – *The Duchess of Malfi*

Timberlake Wertenbaker – *Our Country's Good*

Arnold Wesker – *Chicken Soup With Barley*

Oscar Wilde – *The Importance Of Being Earnest*

Thornton Wilder – *Our Town*

Tennessee Williams – *A Streetcar Named Desire*

Esther Wilson – *Ten Tiny Toes*

Kim Wiltshire and Paul Hine – *Project XXX (if you want to a read a play by the person writing this book!)*

Michael Wynne – *The Knocky*

Other than plays, there are useful books about theatre for the new play-wright to read, which I've split into what I would call 'craft texts', that is books that explore what it means to write for theatre or how theatre works as well as general creative writing craft texts, and theatre history books. Again, this is not a definitive list, so please research further. I have included some of my favourites here as well as texts mentioned in the book.

Craft texts

Aristotle. (1996). *Poetics*. London: Penguin Classics (amongst many other editions).

Antonin Artaud. (2010). *Theatre and Its Double*. Surrey: Oneworld Classics.

Alan Ayckbourne. (2004). *The Crafty Art of Playmaking*. London: Faber and Faber.

David Ball. (1983). *Backwards and Forwards: A Technical Manual for Reading Plays*. Carbondale: Southern Illinois University Press.

Craig Batty and Zara Waldeback. (2008). *Writing for the Screen: Creative and Critical Approaches*. Basingstoke: Palgrave Macmillan.

Amanda Boulter. (2007). *Writing Fiction: Creative and Critical Approaches.* Basingstoke: Palgrave Macmillan.

Peter Brook. (2008). *The Empty Space.* London: Penguin Classics.

Ken Dancyger and Jeff Rush. (2013). *Alternative Scriptwriting: Beyond the Hollywood Formula.* Burlington: Focal Press.

David Edgar. (2009). *How Plays Work.* London: Nick Hern Books.

Sid Field. (2005). *Screenplay: The Foundations of Screenwriting.* New York: Delta.

Tim Fountain. (2007). *So You Want to be a Playwright.* London: Nick Hern Books.

Baz Kershaw and Tony Coult. (1983). *Engineers of Imagination: Welfare State Handbook.* London: Bloomsbury.

Ruth Little and Emily McLaughlin. (2007). *The Royal Court Theatre: Inside Out.* London: Oberon Books.

David Mamet. (2007). *Three Uses of the Knife.* London: Methuen.

John McGrath. (1981). *A Good Night Out.* London: Methuen Drama.

Robert McKee. (1999). *Story: Substance, Structure, Style and the Principles of Screenwriting.* London: Methuen.

Duska Radosavljevic. (2013). *Theatre-Making: Interplay between Text and Performance in the 21st Century.* Basingstoke: Palgrave Macmillan.

Blake Snyder. (2005). *Save the Cat.* Studio City, CA: Michael Wiese Productions.

Stuart Spencer. (2003). *The Playwrights Guidebook.* New York: Faber and Faber.

Cathy Turner and Synne Behrndt. (2007). *Dramaturgy and Performance.* Basingstoke: Palgrave Macmillan.

Christopher Vogler. (2007). *The Writer's Journey.* Studio City, CA: Michael Wiese Productions.

Theatre history texts

Oscar G. Brockett and Franklin J. Hildy. (2010). *History of Theatre.* Boston, MA: Allyn & Bacon.

John Russell Brown. (2001). *The Oxford Illustrated History of Theatre.* Oxford: Oxford University Press.

Michael Cordner and Peter Holland. (2007). *Players, Playwrights, Playhouses: Investigating Performance, 1660-1800.* Basingstoke: Palgrave Macmillan.

Tracy C. Davis and Peter Holland. (2010). *The Performing Century: Nineteenth Century Theatre's History.* Basingstoke: Palgrave Macmillan.

Phyllis Hartnoll. (1985). *The Theatre: A Concise History Revised Edition.* London: Thames and Hudson.

Ronald Harwood. (1984). *All the World's A Stage.* London: Martin Secker & Warburg Limited.

Peter Holland and Stephen Orgel. (2004). *From Script to Stage in Early Modern England.* Basingstoke: Palgrave Macmillan.

Simon Shepherd. (2009). *The Cambridge Introduction to Modern British Theatre.* Cambridge: Cambridge University Press.

Phillip B. Zarrilli and Bruce McConachie. (2010). *Theatre Histories: An Introduction.* New York: Routledge.

Index